Praise for *Get Out of Your Head* and *Find Your People*, Jennie Allen's bestselling adult books that inspired *You Are Not Alone*

"*Find Your People* is a true reflection of God's heart for us to experience authentic, vulnerable, and meaningful relationships. Through Jennie's wisdom and practical advice, she shares how to overcome the common barriers that keep us from finding our people and pushes us to fight to replace loneliness with community."

—SADIE ROBERTSON HUFF, author, speaker, and founder of Live Original

"Deep community is the path to health, joy, success, connection. *Find Your People* will inspire you, challenge you, and encourage you toward the relationships you need and want."

—ANNIE F. DOWNS, *New York Times* bestselling author of *That Sounds Fun*

"You know those books that you buy twenty copies of and then forcefully give to everyone you know? Yeah, *Get Out of Your Head* is one of those books. Hands down. Powerful. Prophetic. Necessary."

—JEFFERSON BETHKE, *New York Times* bestselling author of *Jesus > Religion*

BOOKS BY JENNIE ALLEN

Nonfiction

Untangle Your Emotions
Find Your People
Get Out of Your Head
Made for This
Nothing to Prove
Restless
Stuck
Anything

Theolaby Series for Kids

I Am Creator
I Am Holy
I Am Rescuer
I Am with You
I Am Forever

You Are Not Alone

You Are Not Alone

A Kid's Guide to Overcoming Anxious Thoughts and Believing What's True

JENNIE ALLEN

WaterBrook

All Scripture quotations, unless otherwise indicated, are taken from the ESV® Bible (The Holy Bible, English Standard Version®), copyright © 2001 by Crossway, a publishing ministry of Good News Publishers. Used by permission. All rights reserved. Scripture quotations marked (ICB) are taken from the Holy Bible, International Children's Bible®. Copyright © 1986, 1988, 1999, 2015 by Thomas Nelson. Used by permission. All rights reserved. Scripture quotations marked (NASB) are taken from the New American Standard Bible®, copyright © 1960, 1971, 1977, 1995 by the Lockman Foundation. Used by permission. All rights reserved. (www.Lockman.org). Scripture quotations marked (NET) are taken from the NET Bible®, copyright © 1996, 2019 by Biblical Studies Press LLC (http://netbible.com). All rights reserved. The book's epigraph (Matthew 28:20) and Scripture quotations marked (NIV) are taken from the Holy Bible, New International Version®, NIV®. Copyright © 1973, 1978, 1984, 2011 by Biblica Inc.™ Used by permission of Zondervan. All rights reserved worldwide. (www.zondervan.com). The "NIV" and "New International Version" are trademarks registered in the United States Patent and Trademark Office by Biblica, Inc.™ Scripture quotations marked (NKJV) are taken from the New King James Version®. Copyright © 1982 by Thomas Nelson. Used by permission. All rights reserved. Scripture quotations marked (NLV) are taken from the New Life Version, copyright © 1969 and 2003. Used by permission of Barbour Publishing Inc., Uhrichsville, Ohio 44683. All rights reserved.

Italics in Scripture quotations reflect the author's added emphasis.

A WaterBrook Trade Paperback Original

Copyright © 2024 by Jennie Allen

All rights reserved.

Images: Page 27: sudowoodo; Page 28: adobestock; Page 29: 9bdesign; Page 45: bismillah_bd; Page 59: ~ Bitter ~; Page 70: Marisha; all adapted/via adobestock.com

Published in the United States by WaterBrook, an imprint of Random House, a division of Penguin Random House LLC.

WATERBROOK and colophon are registered trademarks of Penguin Random House LLC.

Published in association with Yates & Yates, www.yates2.com.

This work is adapted from the following: *Nothing to Prove,* copyright © 2017 by Jennie Allen, *Get Out of Your Head,* copyright © 2020 by Jennie Allen, and *Find Your People,* copyright © 2022 by Jennie Allen, all published in the United States in hardcover by WaterBrook, an imprint of Random House, a division of Penguin Random House LLC, in 2017, 2020, and 2022, respectively.

Trade Paperback ISBN 978-0-593-44544-0
Ebook ISBN 978-0-593-44545-7

The Library of Congress catalog record is available at https://lccn.loc.gov/2023046523.

Printed in the United States of America on acid-free paper

waterbrookmultnomah.com

9 8 7 6 5 4 3 2

For details about special quantity discounts, special books, or book excerpts, contact specialmarketscms@penguinrandomhouse.com.

To my kids: Being with you in your thoughts and struggles turned out to be the good stuff!

Thanks for letting us into the hard and the good of your lives. We love you so much, Conner, Kate, Caroline, and Coop.

Surely I am with you always, to the very end of the age.

—JESUS

No matter how alone we might feel, He promised:

He will always be with us.

Contents

Part One

Part Two

Part Three

Power Tools–
Resources for Your Fight

Part One

1

Letter to the Reader

HI, FRIEND. CHANCES ARE IF YOU ARE READING THESE WORDS, the thoughts in your brain feel a little chaotic sometimes.

Have you ever played on a Sit 'n Spin? In case you never have, they are big plastic disks with a handle in the middle, like a kid-sized spinning top. You wrap your legs around the middle, sit down, and spin yourself. Sit and spin.

That is my brain.

Fear and worry constantly bother me. I sit in my anxious thoughts and spin around and around.

When I started a new school in ninth grade, my brain was extra spinny. I walked in to find my gray locker in a sea of humans I had never seen before. They all seemed perfectly at ease in the chaos. I was not. I couldn't find my locker, and no one offered to help me. I started to spin.

Questions whirred around me . . .

- *Does anyone like me?*
- *Does anyone want to be my friend?*
- *Does anyone even know I exist?*

Being a person who always felt like she had to win everyone's approval, this year of school about did me in. Every night as I would try to fall asleep, my brain kept crawling onto my imaginary Sit 'n Spin. I spent hours whirling in worry.

We worry about the things we love, the things that matter most to us. At that point in my life, what mattered most was acceptance, approval, fitting in.

We worry about what we value. I valued the admiration and approval of my family and friends. So I would lie in bed and worry about what they thought. The unknown opinions of a few people took over my mind.

Since then I've learned that me and my spinny brain are not alone! Lots of us sit and spin. That means you are not alone either. (You're going to see a bunch of special sections throughout this book titled "You Said . . ." The answers to the questions in those sections came from people your age.) This is a book about all the ways our brains can spin—and all the ways God wants to help us with our spinny brains.

You are not alone!

. . .

How do you deal with big thoughts and feelings?

If you're like me, sometimes you don't!

Some days it feels like your thoughts and feelings are running wild. They feel huge and mysterious. You get overwhelmed, melt down, and freeze up. You can feel so discombobulated or nervous or embarrassed that it's downright scary. And once the cycle starts, it just keeps going, doesn't it? Like a spiral sliding down, down, down. It's a terrible feeling! And it can seem like it's running the show in your life.

I bet you don't want to live this way. Neither do I! So why do we feel so stuck inside our spinning heads and sinking hearts?

It's crazy if you think about it: How can something we can't see—*thoughts*—control so much? Our thoughts often decide:

- *what we feel*
- *what we do*
- *what we say or don't say*
- *how we move*
- *how we sleep*
- *what we want*
- *what we hate*
- *what we love*

In this book, we're going to learn how to stop anxious thoughts.

The thing is, you can choose what to think about! But you will need some help. Learning this new skill will take tools, training, and most of all, prayer and grace from God. But you *can* do it! Choosing your thoughts is a whole new way to live and grow. Come with me, and let's learn how to stop anxious thoughts from spiraling down and spinning out.

And if you don't know Jesus, I want to tell you all about Him. Bookmark this page and start reading at page 149 to learn what it means to know God. Then come back here! When we believe God loved us so much that He sent Jesus to earth to die on a cross for us, and when we give our lives to Him, we get to be with God forever. He gives us His Spirit to help us.

The Bible tells us we can "take captive every thought to make it obedient to Christ" (2 Corinthians 10:5, NIV).

Like, capture every thought? And bring it to Jesus?

Really?

Really.

Take captive every thought . . . That means it's possible.

2

You Are Not Alone

Fighting for a Free and Healthy Mind

POWER THOUGHT

I have a choice.

DID YOU KNOW YOU'RE PART OF AN epic battle? Not with suits of armor and swords. Not with dragons or spaceships or superheroes. Not with armies or tanks or big explosions.

You're in a battle for your mind. It's a quiet, invisible battle that goes on between your ears. But it's a fight just the same.

Don't worry. *You're not fighting alone.* People all around you are fighting it too. Adults are fighting alongside you. God is fighting with you, and He promises the big war is already won. Still, while we're living in the brokenness of this world, we have to fight through the everyday battles.

What is this daily battle?

Maybe you've felt it. It's all those messages that trickle into your mind, the ones that make you start thinking, *I'm helpless. I'm worthless. I'm unlovable.* It's when out-of-control thoughts and feelings seem to drag you down and take over.

If it feels like you're under attack from all sides, it's because, well, you are.

You may hear a lot about anxiety, depression, fears, and

worries. People used to be too embarrassed to talk about that stuff, but not as much these days. Kids are talking to one another about their struggles. And that's great. It's so much better to be aware of and open about the battles we face, isn't it?

Still, you're under a lot of pressure. Because of the internet, you have access to all the information in the world. If you have access to a tablet, computer, or phone, it's not hard to find out all about world problems, city problems, and neighborhood problems every single day. Add that to the family problems you carry from home and the pressures you feel at school, *and that's a lot of problems.* Way more than you were meant to handle alone. And then, there's media—TV shows, internet videos, games, chats, maybe even social media. A lot of you are constantly getting input from hundreds, even thousands, of other people! So you're carrying a lot of pressure, a lot of people's opinions, and a lot of people's burdens. It can be so heavy.

Do you ever feel like your mind is under attack? Or see your friends struggling in this way? Draw a picture of yourself fighting this battle in the box below, labeling the things you're fighting against.

Yep, there's a battle going on for your mind. But you have everything you need to step up and fight—and win. The Bible tells us,

> Our fight is not against people on earth. We are fighting against the rulers and authorities and the powers of this world's darkness. We are fighting against the spiritual powers of evil in the heavenly world. (Ephesians 6:12, ICB)

Sounds scary, right? How do we fight against something we can't even see? With these special weapons God gives us:

> We fight with weapons that are different from those the world uses. Our weapons have power from God. These weapons can destroy the enemy's strong places. . . . *We capture every thought* and make it give up and obey Christ. (2 Corinthians 10:4–5, ICB)

Let's dig in and find out more about how to win this fight.

Who Are We Fighting?

We're not just fighting spiraling minds and bad feelings. There's someone behind it all. God's enemy—Satan, the devil—is real. And his biggest delight is discouraging God's children and keeping them from being the powerful warriors they are. The Bible says he "prowls around like a roaring lion, seeking someone to devour" (1 Peter 5:8). He "comes only to steal and kill and destroy" (John 10:10). "He is a liar and the father of lies" (John 8:44). He's no joke.

But Jesus is just as real—and way more powerful. The Bible tells us, "The reason the Son of God appeared was to destroy the works of the devil" (1 John 3:8). "The God of peace will soon crush Satan under your feet" (Romans 16:20). "God defeated the spiritual rulers and powers. With the cross God won the victory and defeated them. He showed the world that they were powerless" (Colossians 2:15, ICB).

He's got this battle covered!

To find out more about how Jesus fights—and how He fights for you—turn to the Who Is God? section starting on page 149. If you don't know Jesus very well, that's the perfect place to start!

Jesus will have the ultimate victory. While we are on earth, though, we still have to deal with the world's brokenness. But we get to draw close to Jesus. We can take the weapons He gives us and fight to know His victory in our everyday lives until we see it fully in heaven.

I'm not a victim to my thoughts. I can INTERRUPT them.

What you believe and what you think about matter, and the Enemy knows it. He wants to get in your head to distract you from doing good. He wants to sink you so deep that you feel helpless, overwhelmed, shut down—like you can't make a difference for the kingdom of God. He wants you spinning and spiraling.

So we start by *thinking about our thoughts* and what we believe.

Fighting in Your Head

The fight starts in our heads. In the brain God created for you.

There is much we don't know about the brain. But did you know that scientists and doctors have learned more about it in this generation than we knew for the previous generations combined? Amazing!

One of the things we've learned is that the brain is constantly changing, whether or not we mean for it to. That means we can change our thinking! The Bible tells us we can. One verse says, "Do not be conformed to this world, but be transformed by the renewal of your mind" (Romans 12:2).

Sounds good, right? Refreshing. Like deep breaths for your brain.

If we don't renew our minds—give them a regular refresh or reset—they tend to spiral out of control.

Here's how the spiral works for a lot of us:

Feelings lead to thoughts.
Thoughts lead to actions.
Actions have consequences.
Consequences make us feel feelings.
And then it starts all over again.

Kind of makes me dizzy!

But the good news is, we can stop the spiral. How? By taking *control of the thoughts we choose to think.*

We can do as the Bible says and "take every thought captive." Not only can our thoughts be changed, but *we* can be the ones to change them!

You.

And I.

Can change.

Feelings lead to thoughts

Thoughts lead to actions

Actions have consequences

Consequences make us feel feelings

God has given us that power, and science proves we can. God built our brains full of little paths, like trails that are too small to see. They're called *neural pathways*. Those pathways are built—believe it or not—by our thoughts!

It's a little like making a road in the woods. At first you can see only a faint trail of flattened leaves on the ground—it's been walked down just a few times before. But over time the path gets so popular that someone comes and puts gravel on top of the dirt. Then they pour cement on top of that gravel. And then they put in signs and streetlights along the way. Eventually the path is so nice and clear that it would be silly to take another route. That path is just the path you always take. Those thoughts are the thoughts you always think.

Do you want to take a new path in your mind? Think a new thought! If the paths you've made always take you down a spiral of fear, or anxiety, or bad feelings, you can make new ones.

You can *redirect* the traffic. Put up a sign that says, "Road closed! New thoughts, this way!"

And because *how we think* directly leads to *how we live,* that choice makes a huge difference in your life.

Your Growing Brain

Knowing more about the science of our brains can help us have patience with ourselves as we work through things.[1] Here are some things about your brain that you may not know:

When we are somewhere between the ages of eight and thirteen, chemicals called *hormones* start to act. These hormones are part of the amazing system God made that helps your body grow and mature. Your brain, too, is growing and adapting in this time of life called *puberty*. The part of the brain that's in charge of emotions is getting really active. You're undergoing huge changes in your body, so it's normal to feel a little out of whack. Your emotional system is very sensitive. The front part of your brain, which helps you handle your emotions, is under construction!

So a growing brain + changing hormones = an extra challenge. Like dealing with growing pains, but in your emotions and thoughts.

Part of your journey will be learning what to do with big feelings. Your brain might need a break sometimes! You need understanding and gentleness. We'll talk more about how to take breaks when you need them as your brain grows and matures the way God intended.

What thoughts do you wish you didn't have anymore?

_____

_____

_____

How does it feel to know you can control your thoughts?

_____

_____

_____

The Weapon of Choice

Throughout the coming chapters you and I will learn how to go to war with the weapons that God has given us, weapons to use against things that try to stop us from growing steady, sound minds.

I can grab one thought— I have a *CHOICE*.

We may not be able to take *every* thought captive in *every* situation we face *every* day. But we can learn to take *one* thought captive. Right? Can you grab on to one new thought?

I think you can. Are you ready? Here's a powerful thought: *I have a choice.*

That's it.

I have a choice.

If you have trusted in Jesus as your Savior, you have the power of God in you to help you choose! You no longer have to let the Enemy bully you. You have a God-given choice in what you think about, and God gives you the power to make it. You have a choice in where you focus your energy. You have a choice regarding what you live for. That thought is like a mighty weapon in your hands!

I have a choice.

That means our behaviors or circumstances are not the boss of us.

Our feelings are not the boss of us.

Our thoughts are not the boss of us.

We have a choice because Jesus gives it to us. It's a huge, strong weapon.

Fighting Lies with Truth

What if I told you that all the untrue thoughts swirling around in our minds come from only three things we tell ourselves that are not true? Surprising, right? I figured there would be millions—at least as many as there are people! But when you think about it, every one of our untrue thoughts fits into one of these three lies. When we choose to believe these untrue things about ourselves, it can really throw us off. These lies are:

- *I'm helpless.*
- *I'm worthless.*
- *I'm unlovable.*

Which of the three do *you* most relate to? Is there one you find yourself thinking often?

These untrue things we tell ourselves—*I'm helpless, I'm worthless, I'm unlovable*—shape our thinking, our emotions, and the way we act in the world around us. They trap us. They distract us from the truth we should believe. We forget who our good God is and who we are. The Enemy uses these lies to make us believe wrong things about God.

God says: "I AM WHO I AM." (EXODUS 3:14)

How does that happen? Let's say you sometimes feel worthless and invisible. You might read the Bible and learn that God says He chose you as His adopted child and you are deeply loved (see Ephesians 1:4–5).

Then something happens. Let's say your parents come home, and they're distracted with work. They have to rush around and do other things, and you don't feel like they see you. Up comes that old lie, *I'm worthless and invisible.* So you might get sensitive to little things they do, and you might feel anxious and start to spin. Your parents might become the enemy in your mind, and you start to fight them because you think, *They made me feel so bad!* But really, it was the untrue thing—the lie—in your mind that made you feel bad.

No human, even a mom or dad, was ever meant to fill your soul with their love or give you your worth by paying attention to you. Only God can do that. But until you stop believing the lie that God's love isn't for you, you will stay twisted up in the thought that you're worthless.

Instead, that's when you can say: *Hold on! I have a choice. I can choose a different thought. I can look for the truth instead!*

When we begin to think about our thoughts, we can stop the spiral. We can reset and redirect. That's our hope. Of course, we don't have to wrestle each and every thought and fear that pop into our minds. That sounds like a ton of work, right? We'd never do anything else! But we *can* allow God to fight for us—and that looks like letting His truth take up so much space in our minds that our fears will shrink because they have no room. We crowd out the bad with the good.

LIE: *xyz*   TRUTH: *xyz*

We can invite our thoughts to spin around Jesus and His love instead. How?

- *by praying*
- *by remembering words from the Bible*
- *by talking to others*
- *by learning about the way your mind is made*
- *by trying practical tools that work with the way God made you*

All these things are like mighty weapons, powered by God's goodness and love for you. Every spiral can be interrupted. Not one thing you go through is outside God's reach. *You are not alone in this fight.*

God says: I AM the beginning and the end. I am the FIRST, and I am the LAST. (SEE REVELATION 22:13)

Turn the page and find a tool to start thinking about your thoughts—right now.

How to Use Your Mind Map

Step One

In the middle of a blank piece of paper, write the main feeling you're experiencing right now. It could be good or bad. You might write "anxious."

Or "peaceful."

"Overwhelmed."

"Angry."

"Afraid."

Whatever it is, write it down. Now draw a big circle around that word.

Scattered around that large circle, write everything you can think of that is causing you to feel that way. You might write "School is overwhelming" or "Chores" or "Friends being mean" or "Sports." Draw a circle around each of these things and then draw a line from each to the big circle in the middle.

Keep going until you can't think of anything else that might be causing your emotion.

Step Two

Talk to God. With your paper in front of you, pray through each thing you've written down. Tell God about it. Ask Him to show you what you are believing wrongly about Him and yourself.

Step Three

Look for patterns in your circles. Are you worrying about things you can't control? Are you angry about how people have hurt you? Are you obsessing about things you don't have? Are you sad about sin in your life?

What is the point of this exercise? It's so you can see plainly how your thoughts are telling a story about God that is either true or untrue.

MIND MAP EXAMPLE

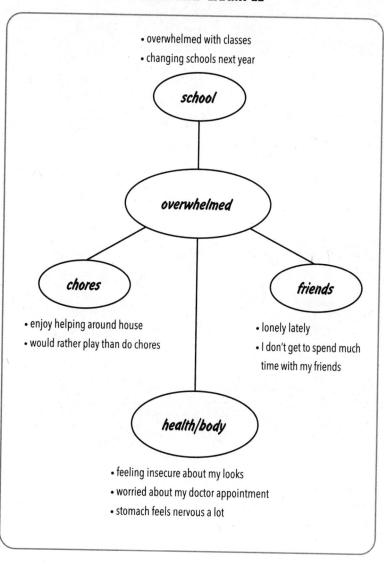

- overwhelmed with classes
- changing schools next year

school

overwhelmed

chores

- enjoy helping around house
- would rather play than do chores

friends

- lonely lately
- I don't get to spend much time with my friends

health/body

- feeling insecure about my looks
- worried about my doctor appointment
- stomach feels nervous a lot

YOUR MIND MAP

• • •

So, how does it feel to know you have these awesome weapons? The battle you're in doesn't sound so scary anymore, does it? God has given you His Spirit and the power, weapons, and tools to shift your spinning thoughts.

And when you're willing to go ahead and fight? Pretty cool stuff starts to unfold. When you think new thoughts . . .

- *You change your brain.*
- *You grow.*
- *You blaze new trails.*
- *Everything changes for you—for the better.*

And remember—God is fighting for you. Your loved ones are fighting for you. I'm fighting for you. You are not alone!

God, thank You for giving me a choice about what happens inside my head. Please remind me today to grab this one thought—*I have a choice*—every time I feel my mind slipping into a spiral. I will rely on Your power and love! Amen.

Part
Two

Part Two

3

For When You Think...
Terrible Things Are Going to Happen
Dealing with Anxious Thoughts

POWER THOUGHT
I choose to give my fears to God.

YOU FEEL A BIG LUMP IN YOUR THROAT. Or a tightness in your chest. Maybe you start to sweat, or your skin starts to prickle. Or your heart beats quickly, and your stomach feels like it's tied up in knots. Maybe you start breathing fast or can't talk. Or you just want to run away and hide. Or barf! *Oh, no,* you think. *Not this again!*

It's *anxiety*. The feeling that something terrible is coming your way. It could happen before a test, when you have to talk in front of people, or when you think about something really scary. Before you know it, you're freaking out again!

You Said...

Q: What causes the most worry or stress in your life?

A:

Grades

Tests and homework

Pain or sickness

Fear of death

Going to the doctor or dentist

Kidnappers

War

Not knowing how to deal with my hard emotions

Tornadoes or fires or earthquakes

Stage fright

Deep breaths. You're not alone.

You know, this happened to me recently. I was walking out in nature, and I saw a snake. It looked dangerous. My heart was racing. I couldn't breathe. I was frozen in terror. It turns out it wasn't a venomous snake. But did I know that? No!

> **anx*i*ety:** fear or nervousness about what might happen[1]

Anxiety is the body's natural reaction to danger. A racing heart, a desire to run away, and a tight feeling in our chests are things that God put in us to protect us. Anxiety is our brains telling our legs, *Get ready to run—here comes something bad!* And telling our lungs, *Breathe faster so we can get out of here!* Or our bodies, *Freeze! Maybe if you don't move, it won't see you!*

But sometimes, anxiety grows and grows—when there's nothing life-threatening around. We think and think about what worries us, and before long, we're sucked into a spiral of anxiety where our minds are filled with voices of fear rather than voices of hope and peace. That's when we've got a problem.[2]

But even this is a gift from God. In these times, our bodies are sending us clues that something happening inside us needs attention. God built our bodies to send us signals that we might be going in a dangerous direction. And He gave us things we can do about it.

When we're anxious, we get caught up in two little words: *What if?*

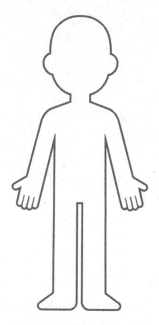

Where in your body do you feel anxiety? Indicate with arrows or circles, and describe what anxiety in each part feels like to you.

With those two little words, the Enemy sets our imaginations whirling, spinning tales of the frightful things that may lurk ahead.

Anxiety says, "What if?"

- *What if people I love die?*
- *What if my house burns down?*
- *What if I make friends with this person and they ditch me?*
- *What if my teacher gets mad at me?*
- *What if . . .*

Feeling anxious yet?

Getting stuck in these frightening thoughts is no fun at all. But there's something you can do about it. Let me tell you how to stop the "what if" spiral.

What makes you
feel anxiety?

Two more little words: *Because God.*

- *What if people I love die?*
  → Because God chose me and saved me, He is with me
  no matter what—even if something bad happens.

- *What if my house burns down?*
  → Because God takes care of the animals and flowers,
  and I am even more valuable, He takes care of me.

- *What if I make friends with this person and they ditch me?*
  → Because God is always with me, I am never alone.

- *What if my teacher gets mad at me?*
  → Because God is kind and merciful and slow to anger,
  He will always help me through.

- *What if* _____.
  → Because God _____.

Here's a lie we tell ourselves: *I cannot trust God to take care of my tomorrows.*

But we can choose the truth. The truth is: *God is in control of every day of my life.*

The Bible says, "The hairs on your head are all numbered" (Luke 12:7, NET). God has got you. So you can say, *I choose to give my fears to God.*

You have a choice. You don't have to stay in a meltdown, even when you're feeling overwhelmed by anxiety.

Spiraling Down

When I feel afraid and anxious . . .

- *I could spiral down and think, God doesn't take care of me!*
- *I could melt down and try to control everything.*
- *But trying to control things won't work, and I'll get super anxious.*

Spiraling Up

When I feel afraid and anxious . . .

- *I could choose to remember: God is in control!*
- *I can be looking out for what He's doing.*
- *And I'll be able to go forward, unafraid.*

Prayer Is Powerful

So what do we do when these feelings of anxiety pop up? The Bible tells us,

> Do not worry about anything. But pray and ask God for everything you need. And when you pray, always give thanks. And God's peace will keep your hearts and minds in Christ Jesus. The peace that God gives is so great that we cannot understand it. (Philippians 4:6–7, ICB)

Wait: Did He say, "Do not worry about anything"? *Anything?*

Anything.

How could the Bible say that? There's so much scary stuff out there to worry about. But God promises that He hears our prayers and will give us peace. In every situation. God meets every need.

The Bible is telling us what to do with anxiety. It's saying, "Hey, don't get stuck being anxious. Instead, do this."

Instead, it says, *pray.*

Write out a short prayer to God about your worries.

Dear God, I'm worried about _____. Can you help me with _____? Thank you for _____. In Jesus's name, amen.

When you take your troubles and worries to God, you're taking them to someone who loves you, who cares about you, who can carry heavy loads. God is with you. And He's a huge God—He has no problem carrying the burden that feels heavy to you. You can trust God with everything you put in His hands. That's what the Bible is talking about when it says that "the peace of God, *which transcends [or rises above] all under-standing, will guard your hearts and your minds in Christ Jesus*" (Philippians 4:7, NIV). Your heart and mind will be protected from that horrible anxious feeling. It's not that we don't have problems; it's that we have a God who is bigger than all the problems and understands more than we do. And we know He's going to come through for us.

I can choose what is true over "WHAT IF."

A kid I love struggles with anxiety. She says the best thing her mom can do for her when she's spinning and anxious is grab her shoulders and ask her these simple questions:

- *What is God like? Is He strong? Does He carry our problems?*
- *Is He in control of the universe?*
- *What do you think God thinks about this problem?*
- *What do you think God thinks about you?*
- *And how do you think He feels about you when you're worried and scared?*

Suddenly, she can exhale because she knows what God's like. She's walked with Him, she's read some of her Bible, and she remembers: *You know what? God loves me, He sees me,*

He's for me, and He's with me. And then she can start to thank Him for who He is. Because He's got her. And He's got you too. There is *nothing* too big or scary for God. He will help you through your biggest worries.

Think About What Is True

After you pray about your anxious thoughts, here's the next thing you can do to calm your mind and body:

> Finally, brothers and sisters, whatever is true, whatever is noble, whatever is right, whatever is pure,

How Do I Pray?

So, how do you pray? What does it look like? For me, prayer very rarely looks like me on my knees for an hour with my hands folded and eyes closed.

The Bible says to "pray without ceasing," or without stopping (1 Thessalonians 5:17). Basically, it tells us to just talk to God throughout the day. And that's fine with me because I really like God. I feel like He's with me all the time.

Prayer can look like me asking Him what is happening around me. For example:

- *Lord, what do You want me to do here?*
- *What do You want me to say here?*
- *God, what do You want me to know about what was just said to me?*
- *How do You want me to react here?*

whatever is lovely, whatever is admirable—if anything is excellent or praiseworthy—*think about such things.* (Philippians 4:8, NIV)

We replace our anxious thoughts with thoughts like these! For just a moment, let's zero in on one of these replacement thoughts: "*Whatever is **true** . . . think about such things.*"

Guys, if you're like me, a lot of what you're anxious about *isn't even real.* It hasn't happened yet! It may *never* happen. In fact, scientists who do research on worry discovered that "85 percent of what subjects worried about never happened." That means it almost never happened. And even if it did happen, the scientists found that most people were able to handle

There is a constant conversation with God going through my mind all the time. Sounds nuts, but it's a beautiful way of life!

Prayer doesn't have to be fancy or official. There's no special script, and it definitely doesn't have to be boring! Just go for it.

Now, Jesus did say, "This is how you pray" before He gave us the Lord's Prayer (see Matthew 6:8-13). You may have heard it—it starts, "Our Father, who art in heaven . . ." But He didn't mean we have to use those exact words every single time we pray. I think the point of the prayer He gave was to show us the things we should bring to Him, which is everything! He says basically, "Bring it all in prayer: what you need, what you want, what you're struggling with. Bring it all." It's open.

My hope for you is that you always feel like you can talk to God like a person and use honest words, in your head or out loud. Prayer is not really about *how* you pray. It's about your relationship with God and talking to Him. Whenever you want. Whenever you need. About anything and everything.[3]

Draw

On a piece of paper, write out the questions that start with "What is God like?" and decorate the paper. Stick it somewhere you can see it, and ask yourself these questions the next time you feel anxious.

When Does Anxiety Need More Help?

Everyone worries. But sometimes worrying can become consuming or take over your life. Sometimes anxiety comes from a chemical problem in the brain, which a doctor diagnoses as an *anxiety disorder*.

If you are to the point where you feel taken over by anxiety and can't come up for air, where it's affecting everything you do, or where you're thinking about hurting yourself, it's super important to get help. If that's you, don't delay: *Talk to your parents, caregivers, or another trusted adult.* They can help make an appointment to see a counselor, or a doctor to get medicine if needed, and learn what is happening in your body.

And don't be scared or weirded out if you need to get help. I've received help for my worries from doctors and counselors, and they have taught me how to understand my feelings and work through them. There is always help, and there's always hope!

If you're not sure how to bring up the subject with a parent or trustworthy adult, try something like this:

_____, can I talk to you about how I'm feeling lately? I feel _____ a lot and think thoughts like _____. Sometimes my thoughts make me feel _____. What do you think I should do next?

the scary thing and even learned something important from it that they were glad they knew.[4]

So, is your worry actually real? Is it true? If not, why think about it? God has called us to think about hope, about joy—to think about what is true!

Here's a tool to help you deal with an anxious thought. You go through it from left to right and fill it in, like so:

ANXIOUS THOUGHTS CHART

GRAB THE THOUGHT	DIAGNOSE THE THOUGHT
What is it?	**Is it true?**
I'm scared that someone I love will get very sick or even die.	Yes, this world is broken, and sometimes bad things happen to people we love, but God loves us and He is in control.

TAKE IT TO GOD	MAKE A CHOICE
What does God say about it?	**Am I going to believe God?**
Don't worry about tomorrow, for tomorrow will bring its own worries. Today's trouble is enough for today. (Matthew 6:34, NLT)	I choose to believe that God cares for me and for the people I love, and He will walk with me through whatever may happen in the future.

Now it's your turn. On the next page, take one of the anxious thoughts you have running around in that head of yours and write it down. What is it?

ANXIOUS THOUGHTS CHART

GRAB THE THOUGHT
What is it?

DIAGNOSE THE THOUGHT
Is it true?

TAKE IT TO GOD
What does God say about it?

MAKE A CHOICE
Am I going to believe God?

Now, like a doctor diagnoses a cold or a flu, give that thought a diagnosis. *Is it true?*

Take it one step further and consider: *What does God say about this thought?* You can find that answer using the Bible or a Bible search, or by asking someone you trust who knows God very well and can point you to the right place. You might say, "Here's this thought. What does God say about it?"

Then you have to make a choice: Will you believe God or believe a lie?

It's always a safe bet to believe God. After all, believing lies makes your head spin and your body anxious.

You can choose to trust God.

Talk to Somebody

As my friend Chrystal Evans Hurst says, lots of times the scariest part of our thoughts is that they just don't go away![5] We spin and spin. What we need to do is *talk about it*. Try to put words to your feelings. You can write them down in a journal or go to a parent or another trusted adult for help. Just get your thoughts and feelings out. Even if you're embarrassed, or feel like you sound silly, let it out somehow. Saying thoughts out loud takes some of the scary away.

God says: I did not give you a spirit of fear but of *POWER, LOVE,* **and** *SELF-CONTROL.*

(SEE 2 TIMOTHY 1:7)

It feels so good to be listened to. So many times when you talk about what's bothering you, without the other person even saying a word, you'll recognize, "You know what? This doesn't make sense. I'm worried about things that aren't even real." You might hear your own words saying a lie about yourself, like *I'm so stupid* or *Nobody likes me.* Wait! We know that's not true.

If you need a listening ear, you can go to a trusted, kind friend, a parent, or an adult in your life who cares about you like a coach, teacher, youth pastor, or counselor.

And you can say, "Hey. Can I tell you about something that's worrying me? I just need to talk it out to someone—no need to try to fix it or solve anything; just you being there is all I need."

Afterward, if you decide you would like their help, you can ask, "What do you think about all that?" If they know God, you can ask, "What do you think God thinks about this?"

Today I will choose to focus on GOD'S TRUTH.

But their help doesn't have to stop there. You can have someone who cares for you walk beside you all the way through your anxiety. Ask them to:

- *Work through the Anxious Thoughts Chart with you. Ask for help separating lies from God's truth.*
- *Pray together over your thoughts. Bringing your thoughts to Jesus is a practice that you'll use for the rest of your life. And prayer is even better with company.*

Who is someone you can talk to next time you're feeling anxious? List some people you trust who are wise and mature and who know God.

1. _____
2. _____
3. _____

Anxiety Emergency Tool Kit

1. Get Calm

Do whatever helps you calm down:

- Take some deep breaths to a count of four. Breathe in, 1-2-3-4; hold it, 1-2-3-4; breathe out, 1-2-3-4. Feels good, right?
- Sit outside under a tree or snuggle in bed with a cozy blanket.
- Draw a picture or read your Bible.
- Shoot baskets, take a walk, or do something else with your body!
- Say: "I need to take a break for a minute!"

2. Listen to Your Thoughts

What are they telling you that's making you spin?

- Draw a stick figure and make a thought bubble, like in a cartoon, and write your thought inside it.
- Ask, *What can I say to myself instead, something that's encouraging?* Maybe you were telling yourself, *I can't,* but be the little engine that could. Say, *This is hard, but I can do it if I keep going. I can take a break if I need to.*

3. Get Practical

If you're worried about something in the future that might happen, try this. Ask questions about what you might do. For example, if you're worried about talking to someone, ask yourself, *What might they say to me? What would I say back?* You can practice the conversation or situation and make a plan.

Give It a Try

When you feel that spiraling of untrue thoughts in your head, go ahead: Say them out loud! Then say what's true.

- *I'm afraid that I'll be all alone.*
  → But God has promised not to leave me, and He always keeps His promises. (See Deuteronomy 31:8)
- *I'm afraid of losing everything and everyone I love.*
  → But God will be with me in not only my brightest moments of happiness but also my darkest moments of suffering. (See Isaiah 41:10)
- *I'm afraid something's wrong with me.*
  → But God knows every thought before I think it and loves me. (See Psalm 139:1–2)
- *I'm afraid that I can't do what I need to do.*
  → But God has given me everything I need to live a life that pleases Him. (See 2 Peter 1:3)
- *I'm afraid of being rejected.*
  → But God has accepted me as His child and will never leave me. (See Malachi 3:17)
- *I'm afraid of not living up to people's expectations.*
  → But God wants me to seek His approval only and not worry about pleasing people. (See Galatians 1:10)
- *I'm afraid of failing miserably for everyone to see.*
  → But God is the best at taking weakness and using it for His glory. (See 2 Corinthians 12:9)
- *I'm afraid about* _____.
  → But God _____.

That is how we fight the spiral. We pull the thoughts out of our heads, and we steal all their power by replacing them with what is true!

God, thank You for giving me the ability to change and to set my thoughts on You. I choose to believe You have control of all my tomorrows, no matter what comes. Amen.

4

For When You Think . . . *I Am the Worst*
Dealing with Thoughts of Shame

POWER THOUGHT

I choose to live known and loved.

DID YOU EVER HAVE A STICKER CHART or a star chart? One where you earned a star or sticker for good behavior, and when you filled up the chart, you got a reward? It felt *so good* to get a star, didn't it? (And even better to get that candy or cool toy at the end!)

I made a star chart for my youngest son when he was little, with a prize of a shiny new bike. Whenever he did anything that was "good behavior"—used his manners, stayed in bed, shared his toys—he earned a little star sticker toward that bike.

And let me tell you: It worked. We saw a lot of good behavior from him! And when he finally got his bike, he was so proud and thrilled.

But while sometimes a star chart brings out the best in our behavior, in some ways it's not so great. Think about what happens when you *don't* get a star. When you feel "not enough." That painful feeling of having done something wrong or failed to measure up is often called *shame*.

> **shame:** feeling embarrassed, humiliated, self-conscious, wrong, disappointed in yourself, guilty, and generally terrible![1]

Shame is what we feel when we're unable to do what's expected of us.[2] It's when we think that not only have we *done* something bad but we *are* bad. That we don't deserve love or acceptance from friends and other people.[3] Shame feels terrible.

As a mama, I want my kid to feel good about himself and not ashamed of himself, but I don't want that based on stars or empty boxes on a chart. Or based on whether he's living up to something someone else expects. But doesn't it seem like people are giving out gold stars all the time? Like when we do something people think is great. (*Hey! You're popular and cool and successful!*) Or more often, they're taking a star away from us. Why is it this way?

You Said . . .

Q: Have you ever pretended to be different so people would accept you?

A:

When I make a new friend, I try to make my life sound different than it really is so they'll like me.

I pretend to have the same opinions as my friends.

Sometimes I'm scared people won't like me for who I am.

We learn to want to win at everything. That isn't bad or wrong; it's just the way the world works. Usually, if we pay attention in school and study hard, we make good grades. When we are good friends, people are often good friends back. When we are helpful and forgiving with our siblings, they are more likely to be helpful and forgiving with us.

These are cause-and-effect life lessons, and they are good to learn.

But nobody can be perfect all the time, and sometimes we make a mistake or fall short in some way. Sometimes that makes us feel shame, and it becomes all we can think about. *Ugh. I'm the worst!*

I feel the most ashamed and embarrassed when . . .

_____

_____

_____

What do you do when you feel this way?

_____

_____

_____

Shame says:

- *I have messed up, and I am messed up.*
- *I'm not worthy.*
- *I hope no one ever discovers the truth about me and the way I am.*
- *I can't believe I let that happen.*
- *If people knew what I'm really like, they would reject me.*
- *I'm a loser.*
- *I have to hide.*
- *I can't step out and take a chance.*
- *I'm a fake.*
- *I'm the worst.*

Notice that when you're saying things like this to yourself, even inside your head, it's like you're talking to yourself. We call it "self-talk." And we can be so mean in our self-talk. Meaner than we ever would be to anyone else!

But the thing is, just like with anxiety, we have a choice. We can choose what we say to ourselves—like we choose what to say when we open our mouths and talk to other people. We can choose to be just as kind to ourselves as we would be to a friend we love.

When you feel shame, what kinds of things do you say to yourself? Fill in the bubble.

Now, what kinds of things would you say to a friend who is having these thoughts? What can you think instead? Fill in the bubble.

And while we can't control what other people might say to us, we can choose to believe what God says about us. In Him, we are *accepted. Loved. Delighted over.*

Are we perfect? Well, no. But God does not work with star charts. He doesn't love you more if you do good or are awesome. He already loves you *as much as possible.* God also doesn't love you less when you don't do well, and He's not surprised when you fail or get embarrassed, make mistakes or feel ashamed. Those are normal human things. They actually remind us all of our need for God. He knows you're "not enough," but He is. He forgives your wrongs because of the sacrifice Jesus made for you. He looks past your imperfections. And He wants you to come to Him—because He made you, knows you, and loves you.

Imagine I went up to a stranger on the street and told them I loved them. It wouldn't mean much to them, would it? They'd probably think, *Well, that was weird.* Why? Because I don't know them. But when I say to my son, "I love you!" well, that means everything. Especially if he's just shared with me something he's ashamed of. I love him anyway and want to help him.

It's the "I know you *and* I love you" that we are craving.

God says: "Before I formed you in the womb I *KNEW YOU.*"

(JEREMIAH 1:5)

The truth is, God knows you *and* He loves you. The Bible tells us there is no more condemnation for those who are in Christ Jesus (see Romans 8:1).

Condemnation is another word for *shame.* God is not about shaming us for what we have done. He's about loving us back to Himself. And because we can come to our God again and again, a God who forgives and loves, we don't have to hide.

Shame Makes Us Hide

I don't know about you, but when I feel ashamed, I just want to disappear. Maybe you know the feeling of wishing the floor would open up and swallow you whole.

Shame whispers,

No one will like you the way you are. Better cover up.
No one will like you if they really know you. Better hide.[4]

And when we do hide and start to feel lonely, it says,

It's your fault that you are alone.

Ugh. Isn't it enough to feel alone without feeling guilty about it?

Then when someone comes along and makes us feel shame again, we think, *There you go! That's proof. Better to stay away from other people so I don't risk feeling ashamed.*

I do not have to fix myself, because Jesus died to make me RIGHT WITH GOD.

Feeling ashamed makes us want to separate ourselves from others. If we're hiding in the dark with those mean thoughts we can't stop thinking about ourselves swirling around, the Enemy can tell us all kinds of untrue things about God, ourselves, and our lives.

Shame tells us the lie that nobody really gets us, or even cares to. We feel unseen and unloved. And to protect ourselves from being hurt, we won't let anyone close enough to tell us anything else.

Slowly we start to believe the lie that we are so bad, we have to do life on our own without help from God or anyone else. The truth, though, is that we are designed in the image of a holy God who knows us, loves us, and invites us into His family to be known by other people.

When we catch ourselves believing the lie of shame, *I'm the worst*, we can come back to the truth: *God made me to live known and loved.* The Bible says,

> If we walk in the light, as he is in the light, we have fellowship with one another, and the blood of Jesus his Son cleanses us from all sin. (1 John 1:7)

Because of this, you can say, *I choose to walk in the light. I choose to open up and be known.*

Open Up to God

We can begin to break the spiral of shame by first *naming* what we're ashamed of. That can be harder than it sounds, I know. But we can trust God is enough for whatever it is. You can always talk to Him in prayer. He's not going to shame you.

Sometimes we're ashamed of something we've done that we know was wrong. (*I lied, or was unkind, or cheated, or took something that wasn't mine.*)

Saying that to God is called *confession.*

The Bible says, "If we confess our sins, He is faithful and righteous to forgive us our sins and to cleanse us from all unrighteousness" (1 John 1:9, NASB). And then we *repent* of, or turn away from, that sin. We don't do it anymore, and we fight it, knowing that God gives us grace and compassion. He helps us (see Proverbs 28:13).

Every time I'm honest with God about my struggles and about my sin and the mistakes I've made, do you know what happens? At first, I feel all the things that I don't want to feel—shame, fear, loneliness, embarrassment. I do feel them for a minute. I feel caught.

But I let those feelings wash over me because the next feeling coming is relief. I get to be forgiven now, and the shame starts falling off me. It washes away in the waves of God's grace, love, and forgiveness. I've admitted I need Jesus, and I'm close to Him again, and we're cool. God really gives grace when we pray to Him. That's how He is.

Here's a prayer you can say when you need to confess something to God:

God, I confess that I did _____. It was wrong, and I'm sorry. Can You forgive me and help me not do it again? Please show me Your grace and love, and free me from shame. In Jesus's name, amen.

Sometimes we're ashamed of something we didn't mean to do (*I messed up my solo in the choir concert* or *I dropped my lunch tray all over the floor*). When this happens, it helps to remember how big God is. He is powerful enough to bring something good out of even the most embarrassing mistake. He is smart enough to turn it around and help you learn from it or help you get stronger and more confident as you discover that you are still so loved, despite the fact that you sometimes mess up. The Bible says,

> The LORD will rescue his servants;
> no one who takes refuge in him will be condemned.
>   (Psalm 34:22, NIV)

Here's a prayer you can pray when you've made a mistake:

God, I am ashamed of the time I _____. Can You please make this situation come out right somehow and make everything work for good? Please show me how to bounce back and grow through my embarrassing times. In Jesus's name, amen.

Sometimes we're ashamed of something about ourselves (*I'm ashamed of how I look or of my clothes* or *I'm always so forgetful* or *I'm embarrassed that I'm not good at something*).

It's hard to be different. It's hard to face our limits. If you're facing shame for something about you, remember who God says you are. Flip to page 159 and read through the section called Verses and Powerful Truth for Your Fight.

As you grow and change, your looks will change, your style will change, and the things you are good at may grow and evolve. But no matter what happens on the outside, at your core, *you were made on purpose, uniquely you.* That will never change, and neither will God's love for you.

When you feel ashamed of yourself, pray something like this:

God, when I feel shame for the way I am, please remind me that You made me with love. Help me see what You are doing in me. In Jesus's name, amen.

We have a God who loves us. We get to go to Him with confidence, not shame—not because we're perfect, but because He paid for our sins and because He cares about our struggles. He wants to help us. So when you feel shame, open up to God. It's the first step to getting out of it.

Open Up to Others

If shame makes us want to hide from others, what's the opposite? Opening up to others. Telling trusted people what's really going on with us and listening to them in return.

So, who can you open up to? To whom can you say, "Hey—I'm being eaten up inside by this thing I'm embarrassed about. Can I tell you about it? I just need a safe space and want to hear what you know is true!"

You've got to be brave to share with somebody who is trustworthy. But you might be wondering, *How do I know if someone is trustworthy to share with?*

That's a good question. Not everyone is mature and trustworthy with our hurts and shame. If you're wondering if somebody is safe, try sharing something smaller—not the big thing you're struggling with, but something you could live with people knowing. Then see how that goes. Ask yourself:

- *Were they kind?*
- *Did they keep my confidence or spread it around?*
- *Did they encourage me?*
- *Did they remind me who I am?*

If sharing something small goes well, you can try sharing a little more. If it does not go well, find someone else—but don't give up.

Guys, people are imperfect. People don't know what to do all the time. They don't know what to say. Give them grace. It's okay. Sharing is messy. I wish it wasn't. The people we're talking to are sinners, just like us. So give them grace.

I choose to risk being KNOWN.

Let me tell you, these are my favorite kinds of people—the ones who give grace. Those who are real about their struggles. They're all about helping and healing rather than hiding and feeling terrible. Every one of my good friends talks about what's really going on inside them. There is a better way to live than pretending you have it all together or hiding in shame. You can be accepted and loved as you really are. But you have to take a chance and open up.

Fully Known and Fully Loved

Shame can make us hide behind walls that we build ourselves. But love changes us and changes others. Love takes strangers and makes families. Love heals hurts and empty spaces in us that we never dreamed could be filled. God is love, and when we choose to open up to Him and follow Him, we get to carry His love to the world.

But it all starts with being known.

When we know and are known by others, we can change and grow together.

So go ahead and open up—first to God, then to others. You don't have to be perfect. You don't have to fill up a star chart. As you learn to live in the truth that you are known and loved, you'll find it easier and easier to silence the voice of shame.

Jesus, help me come to You first when I feel ashamed so I can be honest and real with the people in my life. Thank You for always giving me a way out. Amen.

5

For When You Think . . . *I Really Wish They Liked Me*

Dealing with Loneliness

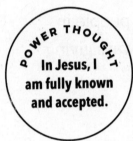

POWER THOUGHT

In Jesus, I am fully known and accepted.

HAVE YOU EVER MOVED TO A NEW city or town where you didn't know anyone? It can be scary. And lonely.

When my husband and kids and I moved two hundred miles to a new town, it was like turning our lives up-side down. My four kids were nervous. I was nervous. What would it be like? We didn't know where anything was. And now, each kid in my family needed friends, tutors, mentors, people to call their own. I did too. I didn't know where to turn for help.

Once we got to the new house, I was feeling sad and over-whelmed. So I just plain sat down on the carpet and cried. *This is too much!* That's when I realized: *I need help.* But I had no one to call. I ached deep inside.

Do you know the ache I'm talking about? Sometimes it starts as a small thought: You are falling asleep with some wor-ries about your future, and then this sneaky thought comes in and says, *No one even knows what I'm going through.*

It comes when you're in a room full of new people who

aren't being very friendly, and you think with all your heart, *I really wish they liked me.*

You and I both have felt it. The ache of loneliness. When you wish so hard to be known, seen, and accepted, but you don't feel like you are. You might wonder if you're the only one who feels that way. Let me tell you: You aren't.

You aren't alone in feeling alone.

You Said . . .

Q: When do you feel most lonely?

A:

When I'm sad

When I'm at school

When my brother and sister have friends over, but I don't

When it's night

When I don't know people

When my friends hang out without me

When my friends are mean to me

When a friend chooses to play video games rather than playing with me when I'm in the same room

When everyone around me at school is talking to one another but not to me

When no one asks me about myself

One of the best ways to relieve loneliness is to make a friend. But the most frequent question I'm asked online is "How do I do that?" Have you ever wondered that too?

I think making friends starts with taking a chance. With something we started talking about in the last chapter—opening up. It starts with being *vulnerable.*

vul*ner*a*ble: open, unguarded

You're Made Like God

Did you know you're made in God's image?

> God created mankind in his own image,
> in the image of God he created them;
> male and female he created them.
> (Genesis 1:27, NIV)

That means you are like Him in a lot of good ways.

You might imagine God's up there in heaven all by Himself on a big chair in the sky. But in fact, God existed *in relationship* with Himself before any of us were here. It's called the Trinity. He is:

- God the Father
- Jesus the Son
- and the Holy Spirit

When we moved to a new town all those years ago, and I was crying on the carpet, something amazing happened. A girl named Caroline, a friend of a friend whom I'd never met before, came to help us out with babysitting. She showed up at our door—right when I was crying! With a runny nose and big tears rolling down my face, I told her the truth: "I need help." And with her big, compassionate heart, she said, "Hey, I'm here!"

We ended up being great friends, almost like family!

Did we become friends because I was so awesome and strong and cool and put together? No! Pretty much the opposite—I was a mess the first time she met me. I was *vulnerable*. I showed all my real emotions. It was a risk.

Caroline could have walked right out and left me alone on

God + Jesus + Holy Spirit = God, the Trinity

God is one, and God is three. (If you have never heard this before, or if you have but you still don't get it, don't worry. It can
hurt my brain too!)

In their relationship, the members of the Trinity:

- help one another
- serve one another
- *love one another*

And this has been going on forever and ever.[1] (You can read
about this idea for yourself in the gospel of John, chapters 16
and 17.)

We were created to be connected to God and to other people because God is all about relationships.

---

the carpet, and that would have hurt. But she didn't. It was
risky to reach out and tell her I needed help, that I needed
a friend. But because I took that risk, I found one. Totally
worth it.

God built ME to need people in MY LIFE.

Why take the risk to make friends? Because people were
meant to need one another. Through ups and downs, messes

and happiness, people need people to get through life. And you do too! (Even if you think you don't.) Doing things together is always better, even if it doesn't seem that way at first.

Made to Connect

Making friends is not always comfortable, but it's a skill you can build. Some people are naturally good at it, true, but if you aren't, that doesn't mean you don't deserve friends. You were *made* for connection with other people.

These days, people like going it alone and being independent. We like protecting ourselves from being hurt by others. But staying in our own little worlds isn't the answer. We may feel comfy and safe and entertained on our little screens all by ourselves, but also, we feel completely sad and lonely.

God Himself said this about the very first human being:

It is not good for the man to be alone. I will make a helper who is right for him. (Genesis 2:18, ICB)

It's not good for us to be alone either.

Why's It So Hard?

Let's be real, though. Making friends can be hard. Here's what a bunch of kids your age said when I asked, "What's the hardest part about making friends?"

I'm shy.

When I get close to a friend, it seems like something bad happens. They move away or stop being a friend.

I'm afraid of being laughed at.

They might not like me.

Some people act like they are your friends, but they're not.

Not knowing what to say.

When everyone already knows each other.

I'm worried they don't like the same things as me, or they think I'm weird.

Getting them to like you.

Getting to the part where I can be my weird self.

It's hard to know who is real and fake. Some kids act one way at church and totally differently at school.

They are always on phones.

What do *you* think is the hardest part about making friends?

_____

_____

_____

What do you think a good friend is like?

_____

_____

_____

How can you be a good friend like that to someone?

_____

_____

_____

There's no question—making friends can be awkward. And it hurts bad when the friendship doesn't work out. Here are two things I've learned:

1. People make up the best parts of life.
2. People make up the most painful parts of life.

Both these things are true at the same time.

Guys, let me tell you, nothing has helped me more in friendship than realizing these simple truths:

- *You will disappoint me.*
- *I will disappoint you.*
- *People disappoint each other.*
- *God will never disappoint us.*

We still need people, even if we're not perfect. Together, we go to God. Together, we encourage and help one another. Together, we grow.

When has a friend hurt your feelings? When have you hurt someone else's? How might you both be able to learn and grow from what happened?

_____

_____

_____

God, please teach me how to break out of loneliness by being a better friend, and help me find good friends. Fill me with bravery and Your Spirit as I reach out and connect with those You've put in my life. In Jesus's name, amen.

So, How Do I Make Friends?

Here are my tried-and-tested friend-making techniques. Honestly, some of them will feel awkward to do. That's okay! Awkward means you're taking a chance (and fighting back against the lonely feelings). If it doesn't work out, you can try again with someone else. You *will* eventually find your people if you keep putting yourself out there. (For even more help with making and being friends, check out the Making Friends Toolbox starting on page 131.)

Go first. Sometimes we have to go first to make a friend—and we have to be the kind of friend we want to have. Quit waiting around for people to ask you to be their friend! You go first! Someone may be waiting for someone like you. So move past the fear. Ask someone to play at recess or sit by you at lunch. Assume they want to be your friend.

I can be *BOLD* and *BRAVE* enough to take a *RISK* and make a friend.

Listen and ask deep questions. Are you a good listener? Often instead of listening while someone's talking, we're thinking about how we're going to respond. But good conversation is not about thinking of something to say next. Listening helps us understand and love others. Ask people the questions you wish they'd ask you—open-ended questions that can't be answered with a yes or no. Ask with curiosity and care for someone's story.

Tell people you are thankful for them. Say it as soon as you think it. A good friend looks for God in your life and tells you where they see Him showing up and changing you. Look a new friend in the eye this week and tell them one way you see God in their life and why you're thankful for that.

Share the real stuff. The Bible asks us to tell the truth. We can do this with friendships by being the "real" us and letting peo-

What Makes a Good Friend?

Available: Look for people who say yes and show up, who respond to you when you reach out to them, even when they're busy.

Humble: They don't think too highly of themselves, and they consider others! When you're spending time together, they are quick to ask what you want to do and don't just go their own way. They ask you questions about you!

Real: Look for someone who refuses to hide, someone who will say what's really going on. Watch for people who will say the hard, messy truth rather than a squeaky-clean version that makes them look good.

Mature: A mature person can control their temper, is kind to others, and loves and knows God. You can see evidence of their love for God in the way they live!

What Makes a Bad Friend?

The writers of the Bible weren't afraid to warn us against making friends with unhealthy people (see Philippians 3:19). That means people who are comfortable in their sin and bad choices, people who mistakenly believe that they don't need to change—those should not be the ones who make up your inner circle. Neither should those who constantly say mean things to you, or about others, or who seem to enjoy hurting people or causing trouble. Run—don't walk—away from toxic people who will lead you into sin and away from God.

ple be the "real" them. Next time you're with someone, commit to being honest in everything you say. Tell someone what you're struggling with this week, even if it's uncomfortable.

Talk about Jesus. What could matter more than this?! When we're talking about Jesus and how He's moving in our lives, our friendships are built on something that lasts. We get to see God in others, and He gets bigger and more beautiful to us. Start a conversation with a friend by asking, "Who is Jesus to you? What do you think He's like?"

Be quick to forgive. We hurt one another. We let one another down. We disagree. We are human and flawed—even those who know God. Accepting that fact lets us have grace for every other person who comes into our lives. Consider where you might be holding on to any sadness and anger from a friend who hurt you. Pray. Then move toward loving and working it out with that person today.

Be okay with having only a few friends. It's impossible to have tons of deep relationships. Love takes effort, time, and commitment. We just don't have the time and space to go deep with everyone. So seek to become close, on purpose, with a few.

> **tox*ic:** poisonous, harmful, having a negative effect[2]

Am I a Bad Friend?

We all want to become life-giving friends, but I think sometimes by accident we slip up and act like the opposite: life-stealing friends. So, just in case we have picked up bad habits, here are some things to watch out for. If you're a life-stealing friend, you might:

- *wait for friends to call you instead of going first*
- *have lots of opinions about your friends' lives*

- *assume your friends are mad at you*
- *talk about your friends to other people in a concerned way*
- *hide your hurts and never share them*
- *remember and hold on to friends' mistakes*

If any of these sound like you, don't worry. Just go back to the "good friends" list. Ask God and a trusted adult to help you build good-friend habits and leave the bad-friend ones behind.

A Word on Toxic Relationships

A *toxic* friendship or relationship is one that seems to drain the life out of us. When we find ourselves in a toxic relationship, what do we do? My friend Dr. John Townsend has some good advice about that. He reminded me that while the Bible says to be kind, it also says to guard our hearts.

Above all else, guard your heart,
    for everything you do flows from it.
    (Proverbs 4:23, NIV)

Dr. Townsend explains that without guarding our hearts, we will be of no use to anyone. In other words, any relationship that drains you faster than it pours into you isn't a friendship; it's a ministry opportunity.[3] True story. These are people who need your prayers, not your deep friendship and personal time.

Sometimes we need to set *boundaries,* or limits, in a friendship. Sometimes that means we have very little contact with another person. If it feels like someone is crushing you inside, then it's time to find a new friend. Yes, we are to forgive and be loving, but that doesn't mean allowing toxic relationships to turn *us* toxic. We need to be guarded about who we bring into our lives in a deep way.

So what do you do when you think a friendship may be toxic?

- *Own your part and your mistakes. (Have I done something to make this friendship go sour?)*
- *Seek to work things out more than once. (Can I work it out with them? Do they want to work on problems with me?)*
- *Don't be afraid to move on if nothing changes.*

When you realize it's time to move on from a friend, I challenge you to be honest and clear, not ghost them. If you're not super close to the friend, you can slowly back away and limit time with them. But if the friend has been a big part of your life, be honest. Because an honest conversation about why the friendship needs to end could cause them to grow. Or it could even repair the friendship. Who knows?

Remember: Ending a friendship every time we run into a problem isn't healthy either. So pray about it. Listen and look at what's going on around you. Ask for advice. And guard your heart.

Choose friends who will fight for you, friends who will fight with you, and friends who are as committed as you are to fighting for a peaceful mind and heart.

Pray for it. Ask God right now for friends like this. He can bring these people to you in unexpected ways. Believe that He can and wants to bless you with people to do life with.

And *become it.* We can't have what we aren't willing to become. So work on being a life-giving friend!

God, thank You that You want to bless me with life-giving friends. Please help me find those friends, and please help me become the kind of friend I want to have. And God, please give me wisdom in figuring out what to do when a friendship needs to end. Help me be kind, strong, and protective of the heart You gave me. Amen.

6

For When You Think... *I Have No Control*

Dealing with Helpless and Overwhelmed Thoughts

POWER THOUGHT

I can trust God to be God and deliver all I need.

OVERWHELMED. THAT CAN FEEL LIKE drowning in big feelings and things we can't control. It can make us feel helpless. It's kind of like something that happened to me at camp when I was eleven—something I remember to this day.

I was in the middle of a lake in an itty-bitty plastic sailboat, with three other eleven-year-olds. We were happily sailing along when some big, dark clouds rolled in. Pretty soon we were in a wild storm. Rain was gushing down, and the wind was blowing, sloshing water over the sides of the sailboat. We panicked! I was in charge of the ropes that controlled the speed on the sailboat, and somehow, I got knocked overboard. I realized I was tangled in the ropes.

I remember the darkness of the water as the boat dragged me through it. I could not get untangled, and the boat could not stop. The power of the wind was so strong that I would come up for air for only a second, and then I would have to go back under the dark water and be dragged along. I wasn't strong enough to pull the ropes off.

The boat was pulling me faster and faster, and I kept trying to come up to the surface so I could breathe. I have never felt so helpless. I thought I was a goner—and I very nearly was.

Thankfully, a counselor saw what was happening, kayaked over, and jumped in and untangled me. He saved my life! He's basically a hero.

I don't tell you this story to scare you or to put you off sail-boating at camp. (But by all means, safety first, and stay close to your counselors!) I tell it because you might know that same feeling of being dragged under by everything going on in your life. Life is pulling you faster and faster, and you keep trying to come up for air. You are being dragged along by schedules, demands, grown-ups telling you what to do, homework, and things you can't control. It's enough to make anyone want to give up—or to freak out and thrash around and hurt themselves even more.

But remember that camp counselor? Someone had to save me. I couldn't save myself. Someone had to give me a way out and help me untangle.

Jesus is that hero for us. He rescues us when we're over-whelmed and feeling helpless. And He gives us lots of tools to help us when it feels like the dark clouds are rolling in and we're losing control of our little sailboats.

You Said . . .

Q: **What overwhelms you the most in your life?**

A:

Not knowing what is coming next

Not having all the information I need

Schoolwork

When my mom tries to help and doesn't
   give me enough time to do things on
   my own
When I feel like nothing I do matters
Worry
Trying to do too much at once
When too many people are talking
   to me at the same time
Dealing with change
Frustration
When I am short on time
Other people's hurtful choices
The unknown
How big the world is
All the things happening
   at once

When do you feel most overwhelmed? We all tend to get overwhelmed when we're faced with a few particular thoughts:

- *This is new, and I don't know what to expect.*
- *This is completely unpredictable: I couldn't have known this was going to happen!*
- *I can't do this—it's beyond my ability.*
- *I have no say over this, and I don't like it!*[1]

These thoughts are enough to make anyone feel stressed out! So what can you do when you feel backed into a corner or so maxed out your head might pop?

Remember what you can control.

So many things *are* out of your control. We can't control others. We can't control many things that happen around us. As a kid, you are living under the authority of adults who make lots of decisions for you. But there are a few things you can *always* control:

- *your actions*
- *your reactions*
- *your thoughts*
- *your attitude*

So much of the time, feelings of helplessness come from not realizing that we are responsible for ourselves. When we start to believe that we are victims of what's going on around us, of our thoughts, of our feelings, of our situations—that is when we become frozen in place. We become defeated. We become sad, sad, sad. Or mad, mad, mad.

I want you to remember that you are *not* helpless. Yes, you are young. But you are responsible for yourself—right now.

When you begin to sink beneath the waves of helplessness and hopelessness, remember that the Bible says this:

We are more than conquerors through him who loved us. For I am convinced that neither death nor life, neither angels nor demons, neither the present nor the future, nor any powers, neither height nor depth, nor anything else in all creation, will be able to separate us from the love of God that is in Christ Jesus our Lord. (Romans 8:37–39, NIV)

More than conquerors? Awesome! And nothing can sepa-rate us from Jesus, who is ready to paddle up to us in any cir-cumstance and save us with His love. He is *never* far away. You may feel like you're going to get swept away, but He's holding you tight. And He's given you options.

Remind yourself:

- I have control over my actions.
- I have control over my thoughts.
- I have control over my attitude.
- I have control over how I respond and the words I say to myself and others.[2]
- Jesus has made me more than a conqueror, and nothing can separate me from Him.

Put Words to What's Overwhelming You

We've talked a lot in this book about noticing our thoughts. This time, I want you to notice what's going on around you first.

What's happening that's making me feel overwhelmed/helpless/hopeless?

- Everyone's talking to me at once.
- I have too much to do and not enough time.
- I'm expected to do something I can't do, and I'm embarrassed.
- I don't know what's going to happen next, and I'm afraid.

What's the last thing that happened to overwhelm you? What was your thought about it?

_____

_____

_____

It's important that you notice your frustration. Once you've figured out what's going on, follow the steps below. (You might notice that these are similar to the strategies for dealing with anxious thoughts! These steps work for both situations.)

Ask: Is This Overwhelming Thing a "For Now" Situation?

Take a look at your thoughts. I'm not going to ask you to just think happy thoughts—but I do want you to think realistic ones. Here's an example of how someone thinks realistic thoughts. Do you remember when you were five years old? Let's say you couldn't do subtraction then. Maybe you wanted to be able to do your older brother's homework or do the same game he was doing with subtraction problems. But you couldn't do it! Frustrating! Now, you might say to that five-year-old, "You can't do that—*yet.*" In a couple of years that little tyke is going to be able to do subtraction, just not right now.[3] So, is this frustrating situation you're in a "for now" situation?[4] Add "for now" to whatever overwhelms you and see how that changes things. For example:

- *I can't do it—for now.*
- *Everything's coming at me at once—for now.*
- *My parents are making me do something I don't want to—for now.*[5]

Time passes, and things change and get better, though it's hard to see in the moment. This is probably the case for what overwhelms you now.[6] How does that change the way you look at this situation?

> Look at your overwhelming thought above. Does adding "for now" make a difference? _____, *for now*.

Take Action

Remember, we have an enemy. And he would love for us to melt down, to freak out, to freeze, to just sit there and feel sorry for ourselves or think, *I'm completely helpless*. But you can *do something*.

Take a Break

Do you need to take a few deep breaths? Step away from the situation and go into a quiet place? Ask for a break, or give yourself permission to take one. Close your eyes and breathe. Go to the bathroom. Get a drink of water. Remember what you can control (look over the list above: *actions, thoughts, attitude, response, going to Jesus*).

Use Your Words

Talk to someone—a parent or friend—about what's bothering you, or write about it in your journal. Get it off your chest.

Decide What to Do

Take your overwhelmed thought and see what little thing you can do to break yourself out of the freak-out cycle. Think of a response that starts with "But I can . . ." It can be just one tiny thing, but even one tiny thing will help you out.[7] You may think:

- *I've got too much to do,*
    - → *but I can* set a timer and do one thing at a time.
    - → *but I can* ask for help or ask a parent or a teacher if there's something I can skip for now.
- *People are talking at me all at the same time,*
    - → *but I can* hold up my hand and say, "One at a time, please!"
    - → *but I can* take a bathroom break or step away for a moment.
- *I feel like nothing I do matters,*
    - → *but I can* always pray, and that matters.
    - → *but I can* be kind, and that matters.
    - → *but I can* serve Jesus, and that matters most of all.

What small action can you take the next time you have an overwhelming situation and thought?

I feel helpless and overwhelmed because of _____,
but I can _____.

Power Action: *Help Somebody Else*

Here's a powerful way to turn things around. What can you do when you feel help*less*? *Help* somebody else! First, it's the opposite of what the Enemy wants.

The Enemy wants us to believe we can't make a difference in the big story of life because there's just too much to do.

When you're thinking about others and acting for them, you don't have as much time to think about yourself. You don't have time to think about your problems so much. But you do have time for God because you need Him, and you're praying for God to move around you.

But there's more! There's a bonus to helping and serving. Did you know that people who serve others and spend more of their time thinking about other people have the healthiest brains? Serving others reduces stress. There's a deeper connection in your life to other people, and you actually sleep better and live longer.[8] Our brains are made to serve other people. So while you may think you want to play games or watch shows or run and hide under a blanket when you feel helpless, that is not how we were built to live. Jesus was right when He said that "it is more blessed to give than to receive" (Acts 20:35).

You might be wondering, *How could I help anyone? I can barely move! I feel like I can't do anything!* You know what? There is need right in front of you, and you don't have to be "together" to meet it. You don't have to go far. What is the need in your home? In your neighborhood? What is the need in your parents' or siblings' lives? What is the need in your fellow students' or teachers' lives? What is the need in your friends' lives? Look right in front of you, and I bet you'll be able to see a need. Here are some ideas to get you started:

- *Take a neighbor's trash out on trash day.*
- *Clean up something around the house.*
- *Brush, walk, or take care of your pet.*
- *Visit an elderly neighbor.*
- *Ask your teacher if they need help setting up the classroom.*
- *Ask your friends what you can do to help them out today.*
- *Look around for someone struggling, lonely, or overwhelmed like you, and say, "Hey—can I give you a hand? Want to sit and take a break with me?"*

Even when you feel powerless, you have the power to act—and your helpful actions can move life in a better direction for you and others.

You can replace the lie *I am a VICTIM of my circumstances* with the *TRUTH:* The things that happen to me give me opportunities to see *THE GOODNESS OF GOD.*

Power Action: *Gratefulness*

When you feel beat up or backed into a corner, start looking around and noticing. Notice the good in people, notice good gifts from God, and notice the good in your life. All of a sudden, you might think, *Oh, you know what? Everything is not going down the tubes. I actually see God working for me. I see good happening around me. I see good in myself and in others. I see myself being stronger than I was yesterday. I see myself getting up today and doing what I need to even though I didn't think I could move.* Once you start to notice those things, you'll realize how strong you are, how strong God has made you, how good He has been to you, and how much He's watching out for you.

We can be people who give thanks, no matter what we face in life.

The Bible says,

Rejoice always, pray without ceasing, give thanks in all circumstances; for this is the will of God in Christ Jesus for you. (1 Thessalonians 5:16–18)

You can say: *I choose to be grateful.* You have a choice. You don't have to like what's making you feel overwhelmed, but you can choose to look for unexpected gifts and good things going on around you.

Start a Gratefulness Journal

Find a notebook and challenge yourself to write down ten things you're grateful for every night. At the end of the week, look over them all. How do you feel?

A lot of people find this makes them feel better every single day. Imagine what a wonderful list you'll have after a whole year!

Emergency Gratefulness

When you're feeling overwhelmed and helpless, take a break, look around, and list ten things you're grateful for. You don't have to pretend everything is great, but if you notice the good around you, I bet you'll feel a change inside.

1.
2.
3.
4.
5.
6.
7.
8.
9.
10.

What happens when you choose gratefulness and joy, helping and responsibility? Your whole self changes.

When we feel overwhelmed and out of control, we can ask ourselves, "What does it look like for me not to live as if this is the boss of me? What does it look like for me to, with authority and with power, trust God more, hope more, and believe the truth about myself and about my future?"

God is always as close as your next prayer. Next time you're feeling dragged under, helpless, small, and scared, choose to reach out for His hand.

I am not helpless; Jesus will *ALWAYS* be with me.

Jesus, give me strength today as I learn to control what I can, trust You with what I can't, and serve and give thanks no matter what. Amen.

7

For When You Think . . . *It's Not Fair*
Dealing with Feeling Misunderstood

POWER THOUGHT
I can choose the example of Jesus to overcome what doesn't feel fair.

IT'S JUST NOT FAIR.

You have to go to your grandparents' house with your parents, and you'll miss a party with your friends. It's just not fair.

Or you have to deal with a learning difference in school, and it's hard. Why do you have to deal with this and others don't? This is really not fair at all.

Or your brother or sister got something you didn't. It hurts, and it's not fair.

A friend of yours seems to always get what she wants. You don't, though. Not fair!

Or someone looks at your one bad homework assignment and makes fun of you, calling you stupid. It's not only mean; it's unfair!

jus*tice: what is fair, right, equal, and balanced[1]

In this chapter, I want to talk about what it takes to overcome unfair situations where you feel misunderstood. To work things out when you can. And when it just can't be worked out, to rise above and not let that unfairness send you into a spiral of uncontrolled thoughts and feelings.

When It's Just Not Right

But first—let's be real. Sometimes things are not fair because they are *not right*. We should always fight for what's right. Scripture *commands* us to fight, in fact, by acting justly, calling out for justice, and defending people who are being treated badly.[2] For instance:

- *Racism isn't fair—and it's wrong.*
- *Abuse isn't fair—and it's wrong.*
- *Bullying isn't fair—and it's wrong.*

We've got to fight things like that. In Christ we can fight not from a place of fear and anger but from a place of confidence. Of peace. Why? Because we know who we are, and we know that Jesus is at work. Jesus said, "In this world you will have trouble. But take heart! I have overcome the world" (John 16:33, NIV).

Prayer for When You Feel It's Unfair

Jesus, would You lend me Your strength? Please bring peace and calm to my mind and show me what to do. Remind me who I am in You, and help me see past this moment to the bigger things You want me to learn and ways I can act. I want to grow strong in You. In Jesus's name, amen.

Jesus gives us the strength to either respond to unfairness and fight for justice or learn when to move beyond it. In

When It's More than Unfair

How do you know what to do if something's really, really wrong?

Bullying: A bully might make threats, spread rumors, attack someone with words or actions, try to embarrass others, or leave them out on purpose.[3] Bullying can happen online or in person. And it's never, ever okay. Go to a parent, teacher, or counselor about what's going on, whether it's happening to you or you see it happening to someone else.

Discrimination: Discrimination is when people treat others worse just because of something about who they are—like their race, their skin color, their gender, where they're from, their religion, or anything someone thinks of as "different" about them. It's not only unfair and disrespectful; in a lot of cases, it's against the law. Again, go to that trusted adult and ask for help, whether it's happening to you or someone you know.

Abuse: If someone is hurting you physically or crossing your boundaries with your body, this is an SOS emergency. Talk to a teacher, parent, or trusted adult and tell them what is going on. You do not have to "deal with it" or keep it a secret, no matter what anyone says or threatens you with and no matter who they are. Abusers use shame to keep the people they are hurting quiet. They want you to believe their wrong actions are somehow your fault. Abuse is never your fault. You deserve to feel safe.

Jesus, we can recognize our frustration, pain, and suffering without giving up our peace and joy. By the power of Jesus, we can show ourselves and others that, regardless of how unfair the situation seems, God is in the business of redeeming *all* things.

When do you feel most misunderstood?

_____

_____

_____

What do you see out in the world that is unfair or unjust?

_____

_____

_____

Seeking God's Purpose Behind Our Pain

What does it mean that *God is redeeming all things*? It means that He's going to make them right. The Bible tells us,

> We know that in all things God works for the good of
> those who love him, who have been called according to
> his purpose. (Romans 8:28, NIV)

God is working, and He has a plan. The person who wrote this verse in the Bible, the apostle Paul, went through a lot of unfair things because he wanted to tell people about Christ. He was bullied, lied about, betrayed by friends, chased, beaten up, jailed, and shipwrecked—and that's just for starters![4] Had any *one* of these things happened to me, I'd never, ever get over it. I'd tell *everyone* how bad it was.

But Paul knew something I tend to forget. He said he was sure that everything that happened to him happened for a purpose. That God would make something out of it, despite all the hardship. And he was open to what that might be.

Paul looked up from what was happening and asked, *God, is there more You're doing here?* And it turned out, there was!

The words Paul wrote have helped millions of people. Everyone he met, wherever he was, got a little taste of Christ's love. Because he went through those things, the world now knows the power of Christ.

You can choose to do something similar: In an unfair situation, ask God, *What are You doing here? How are You turning this around for good? How can I act in Your love and Your strength?*

He is with us, even in the hardest times when we cannot yet see how He could possibly bring anything good from what's happening.

Still, when we're right in the middle of unfairness, it's hard. We think, *Does God really have a plan for this? If so, I don't like it.*

How Can We Grow from Unfair Times?

- People being mean to us might teach us how to ask for help and respond to hard things, plus show us how much God loves us.
- Defending others who are going through hard or unfair things can help us grow closer to one another and see how we are alike.
- Feeling misunderstood can drive us to find people like ourselves, or it can inspire us to express ourselves through words, art, music, sports, or some other creative outlet.

How have you grown from something you didn't necessarily want to deal with?

When my loved ones have wrestled with hurts and broken promises, with sickness and sadness, with family problems and just plain injustice, God's plans haven't felt especially good to me. I don't like those plans.

And yet . . . don't we learn to go to God *because of* our difficulties?

As we go through life, we can often look back on the roughest of times and see that they have made us grow. We don't have to like them, but we can gain from them.

What Can I Do *Now*?

When life feels unfair or people just aren't getting you, you may wonder, *What can I do—right now?*

Try these things:

1. Take a break. Take some deep breaths and calm yourself so you can think clearly.
2. Pray. Send up a quick prayer to God asking for wisdom about what to do. Remember that He gets you and understands you.
3. Ask, *Is there anything I can do about this?*

- *Can you rephrase?* If you feel misunderstood because someone's just not hearing what you have to say, you could try to say what you mean a different way. Be specific and try to put words to what's wrong—a couple of times if need be.[5]
- *Can you step away?* The truth is, we can explain all we want, but we can't control other people. Sometimes they just don't want to hear us. Sometimes we

The Bible has an extreme way of putting this:

We *rejoice in our sufferings,* knowing that suffering produces endurance, and endurance produces character, and character produces hope, and hope does not put us to shame, because God's love has been poured into our hearts through the Holy Spirit who has been given to us. (Romans 5:3–5)

have to step away to get calm. Say, "I need to cool off. Can I step away and take time to deal with this?"

- *Is there something you need to apologize for or grow from?* Sometimes we contribute to problems in ways we don't realize. Stop and ask yourself if this has happened. If so, see if you can make it right.

4. Ask for help. Ask an adult or trusted friend or mentor to talk with you about what's going on and maybe pray with you for peace and a solution. They can help you take more steps if there is a true injustice happening.

5. Consider letting it go or waiting it out. Ask yourself, *In the scope of my whole life, from now until when I'm old, and God's big story and plan for me and the world, does this really matter? Is it worth getting upset about?* If not, consider letting it go by choosing to think about God and what He's doing. Some things are worth getting upset about. Save your energy for those, and let the rest go.

What's to rejoice about? Strength and character and hope—these are the qualities of people who choose to grow and work through the frustrating things you'd rather not go through.

You can do hard things. You can work through unfair things. You can become mature and strong with Jesus's help. To do that, you become strong in your mind. You decide that no matter what happens, whether you choose to fight the unfairness or let it go, you will not let it get you down.

You say no to the lie: *People are not trustworthy, the world is broken and unfair, everything's awful, and life will not work out.*

And replace it with truth: *God is trustworthy and will, in the end, work all things together for good.*

Remember:

We know that in all things God works for the good of those who love him, who have been called according to his purpose. (Romans 8:28, NIV)

I choose to look for God and signs of HIS WORK in the world around me.

You have a choice!

The Way of Humility

Our friend the apostle Paul wrote in the Bible, "In your relationships with one another, have the same mindset as Christ Jesus" (Philippians 2:5, NIV).

And what was that mindset?

Jesus was *humble*.

> **hum*ble:** not thinking of yourself as better than other people[6]

Here's what the Bible says about Jesus:

> [Jesus], being in very nature God,
>   did not consider equality with God
>   something to be used to
>   his own advantage;
> rather, he made himself nothing
>   by taking the very nature of a servant,
>   being made in human likeness.
> And being found in appearance as
>   a man,
>   he humbled himself
> by becoming obedient to death—
>   even death on a cross!
>   (Philippians 2:6–8, NIV)

Amazing, right? Jesus had to come up against all sorts of things that most definitely were not fair—even to the point of going to the cross.

But He had a bigger plan in mind: His love for us and God's plan to save all people. He decided to focus on what was important—in the big scheme of things—instead of what was happening. Because God has the real power in the end. When we focus on what's unfair, we give it power. But when we focus on who has the real power, we are free.

When I Think a Friend Is Upset with Me, What Do I Do?

I'm a big believer in getting everything on the table. Don't build a big story in your head that somebody's upset with you. Rather than worry, I quickly call my friend or send a message and make sure we're okay. Sometimes everything's fine, and sometimes they tell me what the problem is. But sometimes they act like nothing is wrong even though there's something building inside. So here's the verse I live by: "As much as it concerns me, live at peace with all people" (see Romans 12:18). Do what you can, but you can't control that other person or make them tell you if something is upsetting them. You can't force it to be okay. But if you've done everything you can, you can rest in that.

When Adults Seem Unfair

Do you ever think life will be so much better when you're grown up and don't have to follow adults' rules anymore? Maybe you think when you're an adult, you'll race around being awesome and doing whatever you want!

But the Bible says we should go for something different—something like this:

> *Humble* yourselves under the mighty hand of God, that He may exalt you in due time. (1 Peter 5:6, NKJV)

And here's one you might not want to read:

You who are younger, submit yourselves to your elders.
All of you, clothe yourselves with *humility* toward one
another, because,

"God opposes the proud
    but shows favor to the humble."
    (1 Peter 5:5, NIV)

Yikes. Submit to your elders? Be humble? That does not
come easy, my friend. It seems sometimes like they have all the
power, and that is aggravating. I bet you sometimes have a
hard time understanding the rules adults make. Those rules
might feel unfair. Usually, though, those decisions are made out
of love—to protect and guide you.

There might even be things your elders are wanting you to
learn from these rules. If you're having trouble understanding
what those things are, just ask! Like this: "This feels so unfair.
Can you explain it to me? How is it protecting or teaching me
something for my own good?"

For your sanity, though, sometimes you just have to let it go.

I can choose the example of Jesus to OVERCOME what doesn't feel FAIR.

It can be hard to keep your cool when you feel things are unfair. It stings to feel ripped off, even in small ways, when good things aren't handed out equally, or when you have to do something other people don't. But we shouldn't be too quick to call something unfair when maybe it's just un-fun.

Here's where you can go to your trusted adult guides to help you tell the difference between hard realities and real injustices. Ask: "Is this thing just un-fun, or is this really unfair?"

And in those times when it's just annoying, but not the end of the world? You can remind yourself that you're going to rise above. Because you don't want to let it torpedo your whole day. You can choose to think, *I'm okay because I'm loved, and I'm known by God, and my future is secure. God is bigger than any of this, and He is in charge.*

So when something feels hard, unfair, and frustrating, do what you can to keep your peace. Keep your dignity. Practice *humility.* And know you can choose to let go of the rest and focus on God's big picture. It's a beautiful picture, with you right in it! You may not know what the whole of that picture looks like until much later, even when you get to heaven—but rest assured, God's making a masterpiece with every little part of your life.

Jesus, please show me what it means to truly live like You—humble and strong with God's big picture in view. When my thoughts get consumed with unfairness, lead me to choose the best way forward. Amen.

8

For When You Think... *I'm a Failure*
Dealing with Perfectionist Thoughts

POWER THOUGHT

Even when I fail, God won't leave me or give up on me.

A COUPLE OF KIDS I LOVE ARE REAL sticklers. They like everything *just so.* Maybe you know the feeling: the happiness and calm that come when everything is in its place, being totally prepared for the day with your shoes and lunch box in order, or planning an outing perfectly. Maybe you study and prepare and do your best for school. Maybe you practice a song or do a drill over and over until it's *juuuuust* right. Awesome. There's nothing wrong with wanting everything to be right in your world. I think God made some people to love and delight in excellence, improvement, and everything being just so—in its place, tidy, and correct.

It's always great to go for excellence in whatever you're doing. But the hard part is that we can't be perfect. The truth is, sometimes we fail. And for people who like things to be just right, that can hurt—and send us into spirals of difficult thoughts and emotions.

You Said...

Q: What causes you the most worry or stress?

A:

School

Disappointing my mom and dad

Tests

Homework

Trying to keep up good grades and trying to make
sure all my work is the best

Trying to do everything right

Not doing well enough

Performing well in sports

Being wrong, messing up, and disappointing people

Wondering, *Am I good enough?*

Doing my best all the time

Imagine you've studied your heart out for a big test, and you are beyond proud of yourself. You've shown great discipline, perseverance, preparedness, and organization. You worked hard and felt great the night before. When you take the test, you think, *That wasn't so bad!* But the next day when you get your grade back—you see an F. *Fail.* What a horrible, disappointing feeling!

> **per*fec*tion*ist:** a person who is not content with anything less than perfection[1]

Maybe you know that feeling. That sinking pit in your stomach, like getting sucked down a hole. Trying your best and still not measuring up. Wanting so hard and doing everything you can to make things happen perfectly, but it still not working out. It can feel crushing.

The thing to remember, though, is that there is a difference between *failing,* which we all do, and *being a failure.*

When you say, "I'm a failure," you're saying that's *who you are.*[2] You're saying there is something so wrong with you that it can't be made right. That you are somehow unlovable because you didn't succeed. (Remember the three lies people believe? One of those untrue things is *I'm unlovable*.) That is so heavy, my friend, and it's just not true. That's why we're going to talk about how to *fail* well (yes, well!) without being sucked into the pressure-filled spiral that says that if you don't do every little thing right, you're the *worst*. In the moment, it's hard to believe, but failing can actually make you better.

Many times, failure can lead to *growth*. Not only do we learn to get better at what we're doing (and sometimes the only way to do that is by failing!), but we can also learn to go to God and depend on Him. Failure reminds us how much we need God.

Here's a wild idea: Failure is actually a gift. Because it helps us realize that we're *finite*—we have limits. It helps us realize that we need God, who is *infinite* and has no limits. That we're okay even when we're failing, and even after we've failed.

Let me tell you, these are the verses that confuse me most in the Bible:

The Lord said to me, "My grace is enough for you.
When you are weak, then my power is made perfect in
you." So I am very happy to brag about my weaknesses.
Then Christ's power can live in me. So I am happy when
I have weaknesses, insults, hard times, sufferings, and all
kinds of troubles. All these things are for Christ. And I
am happy, because when I am weak, then I am truly
strong. (2 Corinthians 12:9–10, ICB)

It seems like *weak* and *strong* should be opposites. But here the Bible is telling us that God can show His power through us when we are weak. That's just nuts to me! And such a relief, if I'm honest. Because I'm not perfect. I'm weak sometimes. So are you. But God is powerful—and He shows His goodness even through people who fail. We can be free from shame over our failures. It's such a magical, different way to live.

> When have you failed at something that really bothered you? Is it possible there was something God wanted you to learn from that failure? What might it be?

_____

_____

_____

You're in Process

What if I get in trouble if I fail, or people laugh at me? What if everyone expects me to be perfect?

Expecting *anyone* to be perfect all the time is silly! It's what we call an *unrealistic expectation.* If people laugh at you for falling down in gymnastics or answering a question wrong in class, that can hurt. But you were brave enough to try! You're out there taking a chance, learning and growing, not sitting on the sidelines laughing at or criticizing other people.[3] That's something to be proud of. We're all works in progress here!

The ones who know and love you, and care about your growth, are looking for *progress* instead of perfection. When you're learning how to be good at something, the real sign of success is that you've improved over time.[4] Think of yourself as "under construction." A road under construction can look messy, with diggers and holes and concrete all around, but that's what's needed to build a nice, smooth highway for the future.

When my kids were small, and we went out in public, sometimes strangers would give us funny looks if one of my kids made a mistake in their behavior. And I'd say, "Hey, we're in process." You're in process too! Practice saying, *Hey, I'm in process.*

Jesus is the only perfect one, and He's proud of growth in His child that He loves—you (see Ephesians 4:15).

> Where are you "in process" right now? What's a hard place where you're growing at school, at home, or in your activities? How have you been growing?
>
> _____
>
> _____
>
> _____

Say No to Comparison

If you see someone in real life or on a show or the internet doing something you wish you could do, or being something you wish you could be, or looking the way you wish you looked, and you find yourself thinking, *Ugh—they are perfect,* remember that they are a unique person. Just like you are a unique person. We all have things we are good and bad at, our hurts and our victories. Maybe you've just seen their good parts. Instead of comparing, take a moment to celebrate that person's strengths, and send up a prayer for them and for yourself. Ask God to help you celebrate your own strengths too. Say something like,

> God, please refocus my mind on growth instead of comparison. I thank You for the way You show up in [this person] and in me too.

The Bible reminds us,

When [people] measure themselves by one another and
compare themselves with one another, they are without
understanding. (2 Corinthians 10:12)

Who do you tend to compare yourself to? How can you pray for
them and for yourself to both enjoy being who God made you—
just the way you are?

_____

_____

_____

Shoot Your Shot

If it can't be perfect, why should I even try? Sometimes the
thought of failing at something can make us freeze up before
we even try to do it. Or we put it off. Or avoid it. Like not trying on your homework, or avoiding performing one of your
talents, or not trying out for a sport.

My husband's college football coaches used to say, "You can
make mistakes. Mistakes we can fix. But you'd better go at this
with 110 percent. *There is nothing that can happen without
effort.*"

At some point, we have to choose between *growing* (even
through our mistakes) and just doing nothing. Between really
living and just sitting there, not finding out what we're meant
to do or playing an active part in God's big story. Sometimes I
just want to pull the covers up over my head, too, and not do
what needs to be done that day. But what could happen if I
tried? Something amazing, maybe?

The Bible tells us that each person is like part of Christ's
body here on earth. A hand, a foot, an eye. And if one of those
parts thinks, *I wish I was another part!* or stops doing their

thing, the whole body's in trouble (see 1 Corinthians 12:12–27). What would you do if your eyes said one morning, "We're worried we might not see perfectly today, so we just won't open at all." Or your ears said, "I might not be able to hear everything, so I'll just shut off." That would affect your whole body, and your whole day, right? You've got a part to play in the body of Christ here on earth—which means doing your best, loving people and God, growing, and learning. Yes, you *can* make mistakes. But the rest of us just can't do without you, so don't quit before you've tried!

You Don't Have to Be Enough

As you grow and stretch and try new things, you'll probably think at some point, *I am not enough.* You know what? That's okay. You don't have to be enough. Jesus is enough—He is strong, works miracles, forgives sins, and changes you inside out for the better as you get to know Him. He doesn't expect you to be perfect, because only He is. Just stay close to Him and keep trying your best.

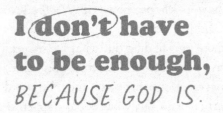

I don't have to be enough, BECAUSE GOD IS.

When he was in tenth grade, my son was asked to play starting quarterback in a big football game because the older starter was injured. It was a lot of pressure, even for a boy who not so long ago wanted to be the real Spider-Man when he grew up!

The morning of the game, I dropped him off to meet the other players for team breakfast. He opened the door, turned around, and said, "Mom, I've never been so scared." Then—*bam!*—he slammed the door and walked in. He was going to go for it.

It takes guts to do something when you're afraid you might not be good at it! Guts I know you have in you.

Later that day, I sent my boy a long text. Can you read it like I'm sending it to you?

Kiddo, God seems to be in the business of stretching us past our abilities, resources, and capacity. It is just past ourselves that we see more of Him, and He is best seen through our lives.

"Fear not," He said, "for I am with you; be not dismayed, for I am your God; I will strengthen you, I will help you, I will uphold you with my righteous right hand."[5]

Buddy, nearly everything you have ever done has been within your capacity. This may be what excites me most about this moment in your life: What is required of you is beyond your age, experience, and current ability.

In my life, these have been the moments that have most built my faith in God. Because as you surrender and trust Him and *jump into what scares you* with all of yourself, you watch God strengthen you, help you, at times even carry you, and you don't remember what happened. That is my prayer for you: that you would experience how much God loves you, how much He wants to help you, how powerful it is to trust Him to do what is beyond your own resources.

I love you and I am so proud of you, and watching what you do:

Head down.

Working hard.

Being afraid.

Doing it anyway.

Thinking of your team more than yourself.

Needing God.

Knowing that *when it goes well, it is because of God.*

Knowing that *when it goes terrible, it's okay because you have God.*

He is in you! He is with you today and always.

If you feel broken, overwhelmed, not enough, stretched beyond your abilities, afraid of not being perfect, I encourage you to take a chance. Break things down into baby steps. Ask for help, like my son did with his coaches. Practice. Do your best, and trust God. He comes through. Just you wait and see!

If You're Feeling the Pressure

Friend, I know you might feel like you are under a lot of pressure. Probably more than any generation so far! You have so much to do, so much available to you, and access to all the information in the world. A million voices may be telling you what's important, what's good, and what your standards should be. No wonder you want to be perfect and might feel devastated if you're not.

Sometimes, though, you just need permission not to be okay. Not to be perfect. So consider this me giving you permission.

And it's not that we shouldn't have high expectations for ourselves! But the best expectations are not about success in this world or getting straight A's or winning medals or looking like a model. My expectations for my kids are:

- *that they're honest*
- *that they're kind to people*
- *that they like and love God*
- *that they know God likes and loves them*

Does that sound doable? I think you can do that.

Everything else is about learning. Because at the end of the day, you need to learn to work through stress. So we have to experience some pressure.

I really believe pressure can be a gift. Due dates at school, big games or performances, grades—they can all help you set goals for yourself and grow. They might feel terrifying, but they sure light a fire in you!

Pressure is *not* something God hates. Pressure is something God gives in many situations to cause good in our lives. Pressure causes our best work. It helps us get things done that we would never get done otherwise. Work matters to God, and we want to be excellent at it.

But you know, you cannot be excellent at fifteen million things, and neither can anyone else. We can't expect it! You might be one of the kids out there playing four or five sports, or in dance and music lessons. *And* you're expected to make good grades. *And* you're expected to have lots of friends and be invited to different things and to win at all of that as well. That's just that not realistic for any human, much less a growing young person.

When It Gets to Be Too Much

Do you feel overwhelmed by the number of things you have to do? List out everything you have to do during your week below, including sports, activities, school, church—however you spend your time:

_____

_____

_____

If just looking at that list makes you want to scream, or cry, or shut right down, maybe it's time to take a breather. Talk with your parents or caregivers, and show them your list. Ask:

- "Is there space for me to drop one of these things?"
- "If I had to choose to be excellent at any of these things, it would be (pick your top ones). Can I let any of the others go?"

Let them know that you're struggling, and ask them to pray with you for wisdom. We all need wisdom to decide where to take the pressure off and where to learn to cope and grow through it.

What you need, my friend, is to thrive. To grow. To fail, and to learn from that, and to fail again, and to learn from that too. And most important, to know that you are a son or daughter of God—and that is secure, forever.

You were made by God, and He has special purposes for you. The Bible says,

We are God's handiwork, created in Christ Jesus to do good works, which God prepared in advance for us to do. (Ephesians 2:10, NIV)

EVEN WHEN **I fail,** **God** *WON'T LEAVE* **me or give up on me.**

Winning in life means thriving and growing. Failing often, and failing well, will be one of the biggest gifts you will ever receive!

Jesus, please teach me to have grace for myself the way You have grace for me. Show me how to turn to You, over and over, knowing You are enough—and You are for me and with me as I grow. Amen.

Part
Three

9

Inputs
Guarding What Goes into Your Mind

POWER THOUGHT

I choose to be still with God.

WHEN MY KIDS WERE YOUNGER, they'd get overwhelmed all the time. I bet you know the feeling (I sure do). Sometimes after school, when everything felt like too much, their feelings would start spiraling. For so many reasons, they'd feel anxious, afraid, sometimes mad, sometimes cranky, sometimes like the world was ending. Whenever they started spiraling and their minds, bodies, and emotions went down, down, down, I tried to help them interrupt the spiral and redirect their thoughts.

"Hey, *time-out*," I'd tell them. "I love you. You're okay. You don't have to panic. You can choose another way."

I'd tell them what is real.

I'd tell them what is true.

Want in on a secret? That stuff is true for you too.

As you're getting older, calling "time-out" is something you can start to do for yourself. It's the most amazing skill that will help you all your life. So what does it take to call a time-out and redirect yourself?

First, Take a Break

Step away and take some deep breaths. (I know we've said this a lot in this book, but it's really one of the best ways to handle big feelings!) When you're feeling at your worst, remember: Feelings come and go. You can choose to stop and be still for a sec. Let me say it again: You have a choice! And the more often you grab hold of that truth, the easier it will be to interrupt the downward spiral of your thoughts and feelings.

Why Deep Breaths?

When we start to get panicked or overwhelmed, a few things happen in our bodies. Our breathing gets shallow, our hearts beat faster, and our blood pressure goes up. The body is saying, "Ack! We're in overdrive!"

Deep breaths *physically* help reverse this. When a shallow breath becomes a deep breath, the body feels calmer. You get more oxygen in your brain, which makes it think better. We calm down, which makes our blood pressure settle down. Taking deep breaths convinces the body, "Phew . . . we're okay." Give it a try![1]

- Take a deep breath in through the nose, and count 2-3-4 . . .
- Hold it, 2-3-4 . . .
- Let it out through the mouth, 2-3-4 . . .

Next, Check Your Inputs

Listen: If you're feeling overwhelmed, there's a reason. You live in the noisiest generation that has ever been. No generation has had to deal with more *inputs* than yours. What are inputs? Basically anything that gets to have an influence on your mind or body. All those devices and noises and pings and voices—it feels like all of it is fighting for your attention at the same time. Your brain and your life can seem mighty crowded.

Our inputs are:

- **Mental:** *things we put into our minds through our eyes and ears (stuff on our screens, videos/movies/TV, music, other people's words and actions)*
- **Physical:** *things we take in through our bodies (food, sleep, activity, medicine, vitamins, etc.)*

And *every input makes a difference.* Everything we take in affects us somehow. Just like drinking soda makes us burp, and eating beans makes us . . . you know . . . taking in inputs through our minds always affects our emotions and thoughts. So next time you're feeling overwhelmed, frazzled, upset, or not quite right, take a time-out. Ask,

What are my inputs today?

and

Are they helping me or hurting me?

That's what we're going to talk about next.

Check Your Mental Inputs

You hear music through headphones or speakers. See shows and commercials on TV. Maybe read messages from your friends or watch videos online. Every little screen or device you encounter is *telling you something.* Some of it's really handy. I mean, you can learn some fabulous dance moves online! But some of it isn't so fabulous. Some of it's a waste of time. Some of it's dumb. Some of it's trying to get you to think a certain way. And some of it's just plain harmful and untrue.

The truth is, all that noise in your life *isn't* just random background noise. That noise is often feeding you untrue thoughts about things like:

- *your worth (I guess I need to be thinner or stronger or better-looking or more popular or more athletic to be worth anything.)*
- *what you need to be happy (I have to have that new thing, or I'll just die!)*
- *your relationships (Maybe I need to do this or that for people to like me.)*

What's the noise around you telling you? It's time to notice your inputs—and notice the things that you're believing because of those inputs.

When one of my daughters was eighteen, she was a total champion about this. She realized social media was a big input for her and her friends, and it was making them all less happy. So she took all social media off her phone. Sure, she'd sometimes put it back on to post something or see what her friends were up to, but she generally kept it off her phone. She called a *time-out* on those apps. I think she saw how so many people have overdone it. She saw how too much social media input is toxic and dangerous. I think people are noticing that too much social media is filling their minds with lies and that it is affecting them—and not in a good way.

My other daughter wanted Instagram so badly, she was absolutely begging me for it. Finally, I sent her an article and said, "I'm going to tell you really clearly why I'm not giving this to you. Check this out." The dark side of Instagram and other social media is that they can cause:

- *depression*
- *loneliness*
- *more shallow friendships*
- *anxiety*
- *bad sleep*
- *bullying*
- *messed-up body image*
- *FOMO (fear of missing out)*
- *a kind of distress called "compare and despair"*
  where you feel you don't measure up
- *declining mental health in general*[2]

Yikes. That's a high price to pay for an app. When my daughter read the article, she quit asking for social media. She didn't want it when she realized that it was likely the reason her friends were depressed and anxious. It's not all fun and games.

But listen. You can make a powerful choice to call a time-out. All of us have a choice about our inputs. We can let noise and junk and lies in our minds willy-nilly, or we can fill our minds with the good stuff. Stuff about who God is. About who God says we are. The wonderful, good, truthful, and healthy things.

What are five things you see and hear that are mental inputs for you? (Example: *a song I listen to, that message my friend sent me, my favorite video game, that show I watch with my sister*)

1.
2.
3.

4.

5.

How do they affect you or make you feel? (Example: *The
song's lyrics are really angry, and listening to it makes me
angry; that text was funny and made me laugh; the characters
on that show look so cool—I wish I were cooler.*)

1.

2.

3.

4.

5.

Call a Time-Out

So, what's the quickest way to call a time-out on overwhelming
inputs that are making you spin? The opposite of noise is *quiet.*
Turn off the devices and the noise. Go into a peaceful, quiet
place, like your room or your backyard (or even the bathroom—no judgment). Take a few deep breaths. And take some
time with Jesus. The Bible tells us,

> Be still, and know that I am God. (Psalm 46:10)

That could mean setting a timer for five or ten minutes just
to be quiet, pray, and listen to God, maybe sitting with your
Bible to read a little. And do *nothing else.* Be still!

Does that sound hard to do? It is.

But here's the truth: Real quiet time with Jesus is the very
thing that grows our faith, shifts our minds and emotions, and
spreads good things to others. It makes us mature and strong.
And it is the cure for too many inputs.

Still, silence can be scary. And it's easy to avoid, right?

Sometimes we think if we can stay busy, we can avoid bad feelings. We can distract ourselves with entertainment or games or noise or conversations or *whatever*, and we don't have to feel so bad about whatever's bothering us. On the other hand, in silence, we start thinking about what's really going on. We have to face it. *Gulp.*

There are so many ways we avoid silence. We keep music streaming. We sign up for activities and all the good things we think we should be doing. We try to keep up with friends and other people around us. We say, "More inputs, please! Keep me busy!"

But in all this busyness we've made it impossible to hear His voice and truly know God.

What's your favorite way to distract yourself?

_____

_____

_____

What keeps you from taking the silent time you need?

_____

_____

_____

The best thing about quiet time is that God *wants* to spend time with you. He loves it! The Bible says,

> The Lord your God is with you.
>   The mighty One will save you.
> The Lord will be happy with you.
>   You will rest in his love.

He will sing and be joyful about you.
(Zephaniah 3:17, ICB)

Everyone goes through hard and confusing stuff, and we all have big feelings that we don't know what to do with. Which is exactly why we need time with God alone, in the quiet, where we can hear His healing, loving voice. We have a choice between craziness and quiet, between noise and peaceful times with God, between distraction and healing.

When we find ourselves believing the lie: *I'll feel better if I stay distracted.*

We can choose to believe the truth: *Only being with God will satisfy me.*

We can say: **I choose to be still with God.**

The Bible promises us, "Draw near to God, and he will draw near to you" (James 4:8). That's a *promise.* Isn't that amazing? When we take the time to come to God in the quiet, we find He was always there—guaranteed—waiting for us. The time-out can bring us a total reset.

---

med*i*tate:

a. to consider or think over carefully: **contemplate**

b. to spend time in quiet thinking: **reflect**[3]

One way to get to know God and be quiet with Him is to *meditate* on His Word, the Bible. You don't have to sit cross-legged or close your eyes. Basically, you can read a verse about God, or focus on an idea about God, and chew it over really slowly. Like you're eating something delicious and you want to get every bit of flavor out. Go word by word and think about what it means. Maybe say it aloud or memorize it. Write it in your journal. Draw a picture of it. Sing a song about it. Let its truth soak into you.

Here are a few good words from the Bible to chew on during your quiet time:

Do you not know that you are God's temple and that God's Spirit dwells in you? (1 Corinthians 3:16)

I did not give you a spirit of fear but of power, love, and self-control. (See 2 Timothy 1:7)

Before I formed you in the womb I knew you. (Jeremiah 1:5)

I have good plans for you. (Jeremiah 29:11, ICB)

The more time you spend with these good inputs in the peace and quiet, the better you'll feel.

Check Your Physical Inputs

Friend, we were physically built for silence. It's like a cool drink of water for a thirsty, overexcited soul. God designed us this way.

Our bodies and minds are connected. God made us so our minds have an impact on physical things like our brains and bodies. And the other way around.

That means your *body* can have an impact on your *mind* and emotions. That's especially true for kids your age who are growing and changing so quickly.

When you're feeling the emotions spiral down and you call a time-out, another great thing to do is *make sure your body is getting what it needs.*

Are your physical inputs okay? Ask yourself some questions about these inputs:[4]

- **Sleep:** *Are you tired?* That can make you grouchy. At this point in your life, you should be getting around nine hours of sleep a night. And naps aren't just for babies! Curl up and take one if you need to, and talk to your parents or caregivers if you need to find ways to get more sleep at night.

- **Food and Water:** *Are you hungry?* Is it making you . . . hangry? Are you thirsty? Is it making you . . . the worst-y? (Okay, that one was terrible.) Sometimes the simplest thing can help you out of a meltdown: a good healthy snack and a nice tall glass of water. (Junk food and sodas don't count, I'm afraid.) Aside from eating three healthy meals a day, go for snacks with whole grains, fruits, veggies, nuts, and calcium-filled dairy, like yogurt and cheese.[5] (A granola bar or apple with peanut butter is always a quick pick-me-up.) Fresh, pure water keeps you hydrated and healthy and cuts down on headaches and dizziness. It's the stuff of life! Such an easy way to take care of yourself, yet so easy to forget if you're busy and distracted. So do a quick check.

- **Exercise:** *Have you been cooped up inside lately?* It's easy to get so sucked into school, homework, and screens that we forget to move. But we *need* movement. Often a walk around the block, biking, shooting baskets, or even a power dance-off can help you blow off steam and rebalance. Do whatever suits you, but get up and move for a few minutes. Exercise releases chemicals called *endorphins* that God put in your body to help you feel better. Nice, right?

- **Connection and Relaxation:** *Have you been having fun?* All work and no play is not good for any of us. Sometimes we need to relax with friends and people we like.

Could you find time to spend with a positive, encouraging friend or two? Someone you like to hang out and laugh with? Maybe it's time for a sleepover or a day out with your buds. Connecting with friends—especially those who love God—can help remind you who you are. (If you need more friends like this in your life, check out the Making Friends Toolbox at the back of this book, but for now start praying for God to bring these friends to you. God loves to give His children good things, and connection is one of the very best things.)

Those are a few good inputs that can help your body and mind balance out. Just as important is to *avoid* the inputs that hurt you and your body. Things like:

- *lots of junk food and sugar (a treat every once in a while is fine, but too much will make you feel terrible)*
- *drugs or alcohol (never good for kids!)*
- *weapons and any celebration of violence (even watching violence on TV can make your body stress out,[6] and you don't want to be anywhere near a real-life weapon that can hurt you)*
- *any kind of touching from others that makes you uncomfortable or crosses your boundaries (talk to your parents or another trusted adult about it—and remember, you're the one who sets the boundaries with your own body!)*

The Bible says,

Your body is a temple for the Holy Spirit. The Holy Spirit is in you. You have received the Holy Spirit from

God. . . . Honor God with your bodies. (1 Corinthians
6:19–20, ICB)

You, my friend, are a temple—a masterpiece. As you grow
and change on your way to adulthood, keep calling time-outs and
checking in with your temple. See what inputs it's getting, and
give it more inputs that honor God and bring health and life to
you—body, mind, and soul.

> Draw a picture of yourself in this square (a stick figure is fine).
> Then around your picture, write or draw the healthy inputs you
> want to give your mind and body, like your favorite snacks,
> quiet time, sports, and relaxing activities. Next time you're feel-
> ing off-kilter, check in with yourself and see if you need one of
> these things!

The Best Input

God not only loves you. He *likes* you. The Bible says He de-
lights over us. And I think when we remember that, all of a

sudden we want to enjoy Him. We want to experience His delight over us, and we want to be with Him. We want to turn off the noise and let time in the peace and quiet with Him refresh our brains and our hearts.

When one of my daughters is going through a dark season, when she's feeling overwhelmed or out of sorts, she's a pro at checking her inputs. When she's feeling off, she won't watch Netflix or listen to some podcasts or play games on her phone to distract herself. She will choose to be with God. And she'll choose good mental inputs. She'll turn on podcasts and videos of pastors preaching the Word of God and giving encouragement. It's like the healthiest snack ever for your soul. She listens to the truth of God's Word because she knows, *If I watch Netflix or play around on my phone right now, I'm going to fill my head with more lies and more nothing and more stress.*

My girl will not settle for being stuck in distraction. She knows the importance of inputs.

And friends, they are so very important. Whether or not we're choosing them, they're coming for us all day, every day. We don't need to be jerked around by them or the swirling thoughts and feelings they cause. Instead, we need refreshing time in the presence of God. Then we'll see that things are not terrible or hopeless and that He wants to fill us with every good thing.

> Every good and perfect gift is from above, coming down from the Father of the heavenly lights, who does not change like shifting shadows. (James 1:17, NIV)

"Father," we can say to Him, "help me see things not as they *seem* to me right now but as they truly *are*." His input is the best input of all.

Stillness with God is the *BEST* input.

Jesus, I want to spend time with You and drink up all the goodness You have for me. Help me guard my inputs and always come back to You to recharge. Amen.

10

You Did It! (And You've Got This)

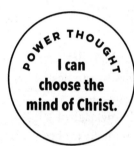

POWER THOUGHT

I can choose the mind of Christ.

HEY, YOU'VE ACCOMPLISHED SOMEthing amazing! You've been through this whole book. You've wrestled with hard questions, feelings, and thoughts. You've become brave enough to think about your thoughts and start to take back control of your mind—becoming the mighty conqueror God made you to be. I hope you've gotten closer to God, come to understand His love more, and started to think about life and your inner world a little differently.

I want you to sit with yourself for a minute and celebrate how far you've come. Ask yourself:

- *What's the most surprising thing I've learned from this book?*
- *What have I learned about God?*
- *What have I learned about myself and the way my brain and body work?*
- *What have I learned about my thoughts and feelings?*

- *In what ways am I most looking forward to changing and growing?*
- *In what ways have I grown already?*
- *How can I rely more on God as I keep thinking about my thoughts?*

I believe you can continue to fight untrue thoughts. You can keep going to God, who is more than powerful enough to bring victory and who wants you to thrive. You can win this battle! And He gives you what you need—including the weapons to fight what pulls you down.

Don't forget these favorite verses of mine:

The weapons we fight with are not the weapons of the world. On the contrary, they have divine power to de-molish strongholds. We demolish arguments and every pretension that sets itself up against the knowledge of God, and we take captive every thought to make it obe-dient to Christ. (2 Corinthians 10:4–5, NIV)

Yeah! I don't know about you, but that amps me up. I'm ready to fight! Aren't you? Here's another one:

Submit yourselves therefore to God. Resist the devil, and he will flee from you. Draw near to God, and he will draw near to you. (James 4:7–8)

God is so close to us as we fight. As you get better at taking back your thoughts from spinning spirals, the Enemy is not going to quit. But keep close to God and the devil can't win.

The apostle Paul wrote this about the Enemy: "We are not unaware of his schemes" (2 Corinthians 2:11, NIV). It's always the same old story. So let's get wise and bust him. You don't have to be tricked by his lies again.

If I were your enemy, this is what I would do:

- *make you believe you need permission to be brave—to grow, change, and do the things you were meant to do*
- *make you believe you are helpless*
- *make you believe you are insignificant or worthless*
- *make you believe you are unlovable*
- *make you believe that God wants only your good behavior, instead of time with you and a loving relationship with you, His wanted child*

Maybe those lies have worked before. But now you're awake. You are starting to get into the Word of God and praying more than ever. God is moving through you, and you are getting *dangerous* to the Enemy. You are getting free in your mind and pointing other people to freedom and peace by your example. The old lies are no longer working.

The Enemy tells you that freedom is found only in proving to yourself and to the world that:

- *You are important.*
- *You are in control.*
- *You are liked.*
- *You are happy.*
- *You are enough.*

Here's the thing. It's like the Enemy promises to make us feel better. But every time we try his way, we end up empty. He tells us lies, and we believe them. We end up spinning again, in the same old way.

But the peace you need is found in only one source. I'll tell you right up front, there is no secret here. Just one answer to your spinning thoughts and feelings: Jesus. He alone is the source of all the things we want and hope to become. He said to us,

> Peace I leave with you; my peace I give you. I do not
> give to you as the world gives. Do not let your hearts be
> troubled and do not be afraid. (John 14:27, NIV)

> The thief comes only to steal and kill and destroy; I have
> come that they may have life, and have it to the full.
> (John 10:10, NIV)

I love that there are no empty promises in Jesus. He always delivers. The more you go to Him, the more you notice:

- *You don't feel so alone.*
- *You feel relief.*
- *You feel loved.*
- *You feel like you can take a deep breath.*
- *You feel known.*
- *You can enjoy life.*
- *You feel stronger.*
- *You believe Jesus more—that He forgives and is in this with you.*
- *You feel the new freedom that comes from a calm and peaceful mind.*

Even if we said to ourselves, *Think happy thoughts! Don't worry, be happy! I'm the best!* it wouldn't work during our worst times. Nothing we say about ourselves—even if we shout it—can make our minds new. Jesus is the only one who can do that for us.

The Bible tells us that "we have the mind of Christ" (1 Corinthians 2:16).

Whoa. What does that mean?

It means when your mind is spinning, you can welcome the calm, strong, healthy mind of Christ into your head instead. When your mind is a mess, that's what He promises! A secure and renewed mind.

Things may be hard, but you have hope. Your mind may feel like a mess, but Jesus gives you a way back to good. The Bible says, "God did not give us a spirit that makes us afraid. He gave us a spirit of power and love and self-control" (2 Timothy 1:7, ICB). Some versions of the Bible call that a "sound" or strong mind (NKJV).

A strong mind starts with Jesus.

The more you know Him, the closer you get to God and the stronger your mind gets.

Fighting for the health of your mind will not be easy. But it's so worth it. I hope you'll join me and other fighters in your generation in claiming Jesus's promise to you—for a full and peaceful life. He will be with you the whole way.

Jesus, give me strength today as I say to the Enemy, "No more. I choose better thoughts. I choose to fight for peace. I choose Jesus." Amen.

Power Tools—
Resources for Your Fight

Power Tool 1
The Making Friends Toolbox

MAKING FRIENDS CAN BE TRICKY, but it's important to try. You're probably thinking, *Well yeah, but how exactly do I do that? How do I talk to people? How do I make friends?*

We started talking about this a little in chapter 5, the chapter on loneliness and friends. Here we're breaking it down even further with extra pro tips.

How Do I Meet People?

Most kids meet a lot of other kids at school. But if you are homeschooled, or home for the summer, or just in a place where there are not many kids around, meeting friends can be more of a challenge. Here are some ideas.

Join a club or class. Start a new habit that involves others. This could be a sports team, a service club, an art class, a theater club, a choir or orchestra, or any group activity related to your interests. You'll automatically have things to talk about with people! What are your interests? Can you get online with a parent or caregiver to look up who else is doing something you enjoy in your area?

Check at church. Does your church have a kids' group or youth ministry? Do they plan activities or have meetings? Check with your parents and a church leader to see how you can get more involved with groups of people your age—and with service projects the church may be doing. As you do, you'll get to know kids there.

Talk to someone. Sit down with your parents or caregivers and brainstorm. Let them know that you want to get to know more kids your age and how important it is for you. Ask if they'll pray with you for God to bring you good friends. Ask if you can search together for ways to get more involved, meet kids, and expand your friend group. They may have ideas you haven't tried, and they'll be able to support and help you along the way.

How Do I Go First?

We're all just kind of waiting around for people to come to us. Sometimes we're lucky and this happens! But a lot of times, we have to go first—and we have to be the kind of friend we want to have. Do you want better friends? Do you feel left out? Don't wait for someone else to come up to you and break the ice. You go first! If you do, people might feel more comfortable being themselves.

A lot of times, we don't want to bother people. So we don't! And we wonder why we don't have friends. But you can do a friendly bother. Hop on your bike and pop by a friend's house. If they are busy . . . worst-case scenario, you got to be outside and enjoy a ride. Risk. Need. Bother. This is what we call *community.*

Not sure where to start? Here are some practical steps and ideas to try. Remember, going first can be awkward—and that's okay! Just take it as a challenge, and go for it!

Pick someone. Set your sights on someone you'd like to know better. Someone who seems nice, open, and willing to talk. Or someone interesting. Or even someone new or who doesn't know many people, who might be looking for new friends as much as you are.

Find an opportunity. How and when do you see them? Maybe it's in class. At church. At sports practice. Or in a club you've joined. Look out for them there.

Strike up a conversation. You could start with something you notice about them. Maybe you could encourage or compliment them. Maybe you've noticed something they do that's special. Why not say so?

- *"Hey, I noticed how you answered that question in science today. You're really smart!"*
- *"I heard you like to help out and volunteer after school. I'm curious. Could you tell me about that?"*
- *"Nice job in practice today! How'd you get so good?"*

Maybe you could make your opening line a fun question, like:

- *If you could be an animal, what animal would you be?*
- *If you could have a superpower, what would it be?*
- *If you could live anywhere in the world, where would it be? Why?*

One of my daughters tried this right after we moved to a new town and she started at huge new school where she didn't know anyone. She says,

I started running cross-country, and that was where I got to talk to people—while we were running. . . . It sounds silly, but I have a question book, and it has all kinds of questions ranging from "If you were a natural disaster, what natural disaster would you be?" to "What does the gospel mean today for you?"—funny, hard, soul-wrenching, all the things. I would pray beforehand that the Holy Spirit would give me the right questions to ask for each person. I remember walking away from certain runs feeling so full because I really got to know these people.

In that big public school, people do not feel known, and they're putting out this persona of what they want to look like to people. And the second that you start chipping away and showing that you really want to know more about them, they take a deep breath and realize it's exhausting.

What a fun way to encourage people to relax and open up! Not everybody liked her questions, though. Some people looked at her like she was a total weirdo. So she just jogged up to the next person and tried again. It's okay if that happens. Give it a shot!

Invite them. Ask someone to sit with you at lunch, play catch together, hit the basketball court together, or join you for something you already have planned.

Pray. Take my daughter's approach and pray before you go up to someone: *God, please help me find the right way to talk to and be kind to this person today. Show me how best to reach out and make their day brighter.*

Even More Ideas to Go First

- Save a seat at church for someone and wave them over.
- Drop off cookies to a friend.
- Ask someone new to sit with you at lunch (especially if they look lonely).

How Do I Become Better Friends with Someone I Kind of Know?

Guys, I'm just going to say it: There is no way to deepen a friendship without a bit of clumsy give-and-take. So how about we just own it? No need to be cool here. If you sense that a friendship is safe, then give these tips a try. And remember, don't take yourself too seriously!

Come out and say it! If you're feeling direct, try telling them what you like about them and that you'd like to be better friends. You could say something like, "Hey—I can tell that you are a great guy/girl. I want to get to know you better. Wanna hang out?"

Serve together. Ask if they want to volunteer somewhere with you. Maybe play with little kids at children's church or clean up a local park. Maybe you can join in a volunteer day or community project or help out an elderly neighbor. Ask if they want to brainstorm with you ways to help. There's nothing quite like helping and working alongside each other to bring us closer together.

Talk about real things. If you normally talk about only light or silly things, prepare them to have a different conversation. Say, "I really want to share some things going on in my life right now."

Lead the conversation. Say why you want to go deeper. Share

something going on in your life. Be as vulnerable as you can because others will go only as deep and vulnerable as you go. After
you go first, give the other person or people a chance to share
about themselves. Ask people the questions you wish they'd ask
you. Don't settle for silly questions! Even if it feels unnatural or
awkward at first, asking people deep, heart-level questions will
always make you better friends. Ask questions with curiosity
and care for someone's story. Find out how unique they are.

Be prepared for rejection. Not everyone will be open to personal questions. Most people aren't used to opening up, so they
may feel like you're being nosy. So you need to be prepared for
a negative response. When you face rejection or get discouraged, find shelter in God because He is our hiding place. Take
it as an opportunity to learn to be content with being by yourself for a little bit or spending more time with your family. And
don't give up on trying again.

Are You a Good Listener?

Listening is key to building friendships. It helps us understand
and love others. A good listener:

- leaves space for silence
- sets aside distractions like phones and electronics
  to look people in the eye
- lets others give their opinions without interrupting

How do you become a good listener? Here are my tips:

- If someone is telling you a problem, resist the urge
  to solve it or give advice. Let them tell you about it,

How Can I Be a Good Friend?

Tell people what you are grateful for in them. Say it as soon as you think it. For example:

- *"I'm so grateful for that moment at school when you picked up the papers I dropped. You're a thoughtful friend."*
- *"Thanks for asking good questions."*
- *"You challenge me to pray more."*

This is a lost art! A good friend looks for God in your life and tells you where they see Him showing up and changing you. Look a friend in the eye this week and tell them one way you see God in their life.

and signal that you're listening by doing things like nodding and making encouraging noises.

- Repeat what you heard the person saying, in your own words. For instance, you might say, "It sounds like you're having such a hard time at home," or "Wow—you're trying so hard."
- Do not interrupt. Wait until there is a clear pause before you say back what you're hearing, offer your perspective, or ask another question.
- Encourage your friend after your conversation and tell them how much it meant to you. "You know, it really means a lot that you would share that with me. Thanks for being so real."

Share the real stuff. The Bible asks us to tell the truth, and this is a very real way we can walk in the light. We can do this with friendships too. Usually, people around us will love us just the way we are, especially if we aren't trying to be someone we're not.

Next time you're with someone, commit to being honest. Tell someone what you're struggling with this week, even if it's uncomfortable.

Talk about Jesus. We don't take a single breath without Jesus, so if our conversations never bring Him up, we should wonder, *Why not?* Friendships that are soaked in Jesus leave no room for arguing over silly things, gossip, and competition, because you're each looking to please God alone.

Start a conversation with a friend by asking, "Who is Jesus to you? What do you think He's like?"

Be quick to forgive. Because God loves me so much that He forgave all my sins, I have freedom to give that same grace to everybody else. We all need God. We can keep being friends even though we hurt one another. We pick our people and commit to them, knowing they will hurt us but not giving up easily on them when they do.

Consider where you might be holding on to any sadness and anger from being hurt by a friend. Pray. Then move toward loving and working it out with that person today.

Remember, it's okay to have only a few friends. If we are honest, it's hard work to love people. Love takes risk. Love takes forgiveness and grace. Love takes effort, time, and commitment. You commit not to run away when it gets hard— because it will get hard. You have only enough time and space to go deep with a few people. And that's okay.

It's healthy to have an inner circle of friends, a larger group of people you're friendly with, and an even larger group of *acquaintances,* or people you know and are familiar with.

Tell Them

Who are your top five friends/people?

What are you grateful for in them?

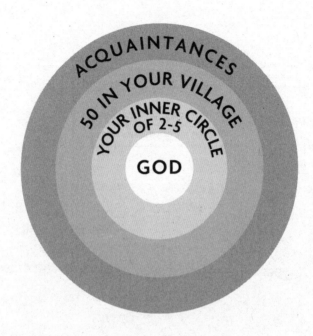

Consider which friendships you'd like to commit more to and let them know.

What are five ways you could spend more on-purpose time with a few friends this week?

_____

_____

_____

_____

_____

Who are your like-minded friends (those who love Jesus like you)?

_____

_____

_____

_____

Who are the people who make you love God more?

_____

_____

_____

Who do you feel safe sharing the things in your heart with?

_____

_____

_____

Friendship Pitfalls

Friendship can be hard, guys! (Have I said that before?) Here are some common pitfalls you might come across on your friendship journey and some ideas for handling them.

Feeling Too Vulnerable

For friends to be real friends, you have to be able to share real feelings with each other. But sometimes it's hard to know what's safe to share with a person.

How do I know if I shared too much? If you really do things right and take chances, there *will* be times you share too much and get hurt by someone who doesn't react well. That's okay. Sometimes people don't know what to do with hard times. Give them grace, and maybe slow down a little in how much you're sharing. But also don't assume you can't share anything with them ever again. Maybe they didn't know how to respond in the moment but are incredibly grateful for how deep you just went. Remember this is a risk, and risky things feel uncomfortable. The fact that it feels uncomfortable doesn't mean you're doing it wrong. In fact, it probably means you're doing it right.

What if they keep responding badly to me opening up? Absolutely, this will happen. Don't be too surprised. This is part of the process of finding the right people for you. You risk sharing a little with someone . . . and decide if it's safe to share a little more. You can also help them out a little before you share. If you're expecting a listening ear, tell them so. If you'd like their advice, tell them so. Maybe they just don't know what to do. (Be sure to give them a chance to share as well.)

There are unsafe people. There's no doubt about it. And part of finding the safe ones is taking a risk and possibly being hurt by the ones who aren't for you. If you get hurt or find out someone's not safe, that's not a sign to stop trying with people. It's a sign that God has someone else for you.

Gossip

So often we focus on the negative, not only in our lives but with other people. It can be really tempting to talk about others behind their backs, even our friends. The truth is . . . if gossip didn't feel good, we wouldn't do it.

Have you ever ended up feeling discouraged after time with friends? Have you ever felt gross after talking smack about other people rather than choosing to see the good in them? Simply put, gossip is not okay, *ever.* When I am tempted to talk about other people behind their backs, I always picture them walking up behind me and how they might feel if they heard my words. Ouch, right?

If you have friends who are constantly talking about other people with you, let me tell you a little secret: When you're not there, they're talking about you!

How can you avoid gossiping with your friends? Sit down and set some ground rules. Say, **"Hey, let's decide we are going to assume the best about each other and protect each other."**

If a friendship or group of friends feels unsafe, then you have no place to thrive, no place to grow, share your issues, your weaknesses, your failures. You have no place to be real.

You might have to have this awkward conversation with some of your friends: "Hey guys, we have been gossiping. We've got to stop. I don't feel safe with you. I don't think you all feel safe with me. Let's hold one another accountable to this." If they don't like it, maybe it's time for new friends. I find that if I focus on the negative, if I talk about the negative, then I will end up feeling and living in the negative. Gossip is a negative we can *all* avoid.

Jealousy

I get asked a lot of questions about conflict, jealousy, and rivalry (competing with someone in an unhealthy way). How do you not get jealous? I hate what jealousy does to friendship.

When I feel it rise up, I go against it with everything in me and do the opposite. If I see something in someone that makes me jealous or wish I had it, I will immediately text them to praise and celebrate them. Every time, I'm reminded that cheering for them feels way better than jealousy!

It works the same way if you're looking down on a friend for some reason, thinking, *Ugh—they are not measuring up.* Let's get that under control. I want you to think of a way to praise them. I want you to tell them what you appreciate. Look for the good. Just that single act will start to shift the way you see everybody else too.

Technology

Technology can be a big obstacle to connection and deep relationships. These days, we have put too much hope in technology to create close relationships. When you're video calling all the time, you miss face-to-face connection. It's hard to figure out moments of tension. To ask, *Why are we having such a hard time communicating?* When you're looking at a screen, a lot of empathy and emotion and compassion don't get through.

How do we fight this? We've got to make time for face-to-face connections, whether it's having a meal with friends, going to the movies, hanging out at someone's house, or going fishing—whatever you like to do. You've got to physically get together and not all be on screens! So when you're making friends, be sure to spend time together in person when you can. Go to the mall, walk around a park or trail, hang out in someone's backyard—do whatever you can do. When you have conflict, work through things in person. When it comes to making good connections with people, make sure your use of technology doesn't become more of a stumbling block than a help.

What If I'm in a Season of Friendship That Feels Hard?

I know so many of you are in a season of friendship that is hard. You don't have your people. You feel like you have no community. One of my daughters went through a tough time like this. There was a time when she was going through friend drama, when it felt like everything fell apart. She and her friends started fighting, and all of a sudden, she found herself with no friends. Not getting invited to anything. No one calling her. She was embarrassed and felt at fault—because her friends had pointed out some things about her that were true, and she didn't really like it. She didn't tell anyone what was going on for a long time.

Finally, when she broke down and talked to me about it, we sat down and figured out what to do. My girl decided she wanted to spend more time in the Bible, spend time with family, and go to God. She started praying that God would transform her, and He did. He taught her that her identity wasn't in her friends. It was in Him.

I asked my daughter what she would say to you in a hard friendship time, and here's her answer:

> I'd say not even having that one friend can be God's kindness. In that season, I remember feeling I couldn't connect to anyone, and it was just hard and lonely. I had to go to Him. Now, when I walk into a room and I know everybody, I don't really talk to God because I think, *Oh, I don't need to. I'm comfortable; I've got my people.* But being in a group of people where you don't feel like you're on the same page with everybody, it creates a dependence on God. You pray over the words you say, and you keep praying continually. You have more confidence because you think, *I'm filled in the truth of the gospel, and I don't have to measure up to these people.* Sometimes I would leave a gathering and feel a pit in my stomach because I didn't think I measured up to who I was around. I wasn't the person I thought these people needed or wanted me to be. But during that time, God taught me not to put my identity in friends and not to lean on what other people thought of me.

You can get through this. If it's hard right now, keep praying. Keep talking to an adult you trust. Seek God and ask Him to transform you into something stronger. He will.

Fill-Up and Pour-Out People

My daughter has another great principle when it comes to friendships. There was a time when most of her connections were with older, mentor-type figures, and she talked about how that filled her up and helped her continue to reach out to people. She says,

> That's where you get filled up, and then you're able to pour out. You need both kinds of people. There's a balance between spending time with people who encourage me and fill me up versus the people who might drain me more. For me, the healthiest thing is to spend half my time hanging out with fill-up people who encourage me and half hanging out with "pour-out" people who I encourage. But sometimes I need more, and sometimes less, depending on how balanced I feel. It's a good idea to learn how to tell the difference between fill-up and pour-out people as you make friends. You need both, but make sure it's balanced.

Add your fill-up and pour-out people on the facing page.

People You Need

PEOPLE YOU NEED	PLAN FOR TIME TOGETHER

People Who Need You

PEOPLE WHO NEED YOU	PLAN FOR TIME TOGETHER

Making friends is a trial-and-error process. You'll keep learning how to do it, even as an adult. As you work through hard questions, avoid pitfalls, and try and try again, you'll grow. But don't quit. Pray. Risk. Initiate. Go first. Ask for advice, and talk to your parents and mentors. And remember, God wants to bless you with community because you were made for it.

God, thank You for friendship
and the way You've made me for it.
Please show me how to connect
with the people You put in my path,
and make me brave and wise as I go
first, open up, and try, try again.
Amen.

Power Tool 2
Who Is God?

WHAT DO YOU THINK ABOUT GOD? WHO DO YOU THINK HE is? This is an important question. Because what you think about God affects what you think about yourself—and basically everything in your life!

Why? You were made by God.

So was I! And so was every person on earth.

God made your body. God made your soul and spirit and gave you gifts, talents, preferences, and a unique, precious personality.

God made your brain. God made your mind with amazing abilities. It can think, learn, and grow. He gave you the ability to have emotions—to laugh and cry.

God *gave* us this amazing inner world inside our heads and hearts, and He called it *good*. After He made the first man and woman, the Bible says,

> God saw all that he had made, and it was very good.
> (Genesis 1:31, NIV)

That includes you! He created you, all your inmost parts, and called you *very good*. Still, sometimes we don't feel good.

But let me give you a promise: No matter how bad things get, God gives us a way back to good. It all starts with knowing who you are and how you were made. And even before that, who God is: the One who made you so lovingly and carefully.

So, who is God? What is He like? If you're not sure, read on! If you know Him already, read on! It's a great reminder and encouragement for you too. Let's start with one of my favorite things about Him.

God Is Good, and He Likes You!

One thing that's true about God is He *likes* you. He doesn't just love you because that's His job. He likes you *so* much. He created you! He imagined you in His mind, every little bit.

God meant for us to experience *life* and *beauty* and His creation and to DELIGHT in it and SEE His goodness in it.

He gave you the Holy Spirit to live in your heart, and *He has a plan for your life.*

He designed everything on this earth to bless you so you would know His love for you. So you would be able to see His *delight* over you.

Think of the very best day you can imagine—that was God's point. That you would see Him in every little bitty thing.

Draw a picture and add words to describe the very best day you can imagine on earth. How can you see God's happiness in a day like this?

If it's good, it's from God. That's what the Bible tells us. If there is anything good in your life, that is God's gift to you.

Open your eyes and look around, in nature and in people, at home or wherever you are. What are good gifts in your life? In the box below, list or draw ten good things that are God's gifts to you.

God Is Creator

God has always existed, and He will always exist. (That always hurts my brain when I think about it too hard.) He didn't need us, He wasn't lonely, and He didn't create us because He was bored. He existed in Himself forever—God the Father, Jesus the Son, and the Holy Spirit. All three have existed forever in relationship with one another.

That's called the Trinity, remember—which means three in one. It's a really hard thing to get our heads around. But don't you want a God like that? Don't you want to worship a God you *can't* get your head around? That's the God we have!

How Can We Know God?

We know about God because of the Word of God—the Bible. The Word tells us who God is, and we know enough about Him to worship Him in truth and spirit.

We know about God because of creation. The whole world He created tells us there is a big and capable Creator out there! It cries out the glory of God so that deep inside we know what is true of Him. He gave us a story to explain who we are, who He is, and what we're doing here so we wouldn't be confused or aimless in this life. He also gave us His Son to show us that better things are coming and that evil is going to be overcome.

We know God through His love. God wanted to love you, so He created you!

We know God through the Holy Spirit. God gave us the gift of the Holy Spirit to live in our hearts and minds. The Spirit guides us toward God through our consciences, through prayer, by whispering to our hearts, through wisdom, and sometimes through other people who bring His truth into our lives and help us. Jesus calls the Holy Spirit "the Helper [and] the Spirit of truth" (John 14:17, ICB). The Spirit is always with us!

We know God through Jesus. Jesus is God's Son, and He is also God. There is nothing more important than understanding and knowing Jesus Christ.

Jesus is our greatest hope.

What does that mean? We'll get there. First, I want to share a little about Jesus.

Jesus existed *before* time. He has always existed, and He will always exist. But when He was born on this earth as a baby to Mary and Joseph, He became fully human and fully God. These are mysteries that can be hard to wrap our heads around, but Jesus was fully both. God sent Jesus as a promise He made, that He would save us from sin and evil (see John 1:29).

We all live in a world with a lot of brokenness and disappointment. We have broken relationships, mistakes we've made, shame, and guilt. We've all been touched by sin. Every one of us has committed sin. Every single one of us. We have all turned and gone our own way (see Isaiah 53:6). Jesus came to solve this problem.

So, What Exactly Is Sin?

Sin is when we choose something before we choose God and His way for us. We go our own way. We go after what we want rather than what God wants for us. Sin always has a bad effect on us. It sucks us in and leads us far from God, into darkness. But through the power of Christ, our slavery to sin is broken. He brings us back to God.

Where did sin come from? From God's enemy, Satan, whose goal was to bring death and pain into the world. He whispered to the very first people, Adam and Eve, that they should disobey God, and they believed him. So they sinned against God in the Garden of Eden, and they went their own way. (You can read about it in the book of Genesis.) And immediately they felt shame.

Genesis 3 says they ran away, hid, and covered themselves. They didn't want God to find them, but of course He did. God wanted them to come out of sin, hiding, and shame and back into relationship with Him.

God's desire is that we would be in right relationship with Him. That's the story of God. He's fought for us to be back with Him. He loves us so much that even when we turn away from Him, He fights to get us back. He wants us to be free!

That's why Jesus was sent to earth.

In the Old Testament, God set up a system: Sins were forgiven when a sacrifice was made, often the blood of an animal. Jesus made the sacrifice for *all* our sins when He chose to die on the cross, spilling the blood of God's own Son. Because He loves us, He paid the price so we wouldn't have to be separate from God. It cost Him so much. So therefore, I like Him so much. I like Him so much because He fought to get us back.

His sacrifice on the cross paid for our sins, forever.

But not just that. Jesus rose from the dead! Three days after He was killed on the cross, He was *resurrected,* made to live again. What power! What hope! Then He blessed His people, gave them guidance, and rose to heaven, where He is next to God to this very day. Jesus is alive! And He is with you, and helping you too. He hears your prayers and loves you so much.

Why Is There Still Bad Stuff in the World?

This world still has sin in it and is still broken. God's enemy still tries to harm us, even though he can't win. But Jesus defends us from the Enemy's attacks. Even better, God promised that in the future, Jesus is going to redeem us, make this world right, and come back for us. It's a giant story of *rescue.*

Guys, human beings messed up. God could've gotten rid of us to get rid of sin. But no, He says we were made to be children of God. When we believe Jesus died on the cross and rose from the dead, when we give Him our lives, we are called adopted sons and daughters. We get to be in His family *forever.*

This new identity changes everything—and it begins the moment you trust Jesus as your savior. It changes our thoughts and the way we think about ourselves and other people. We accept forgiveness from God, and we become forgiving of ourselves and others. We are free to love and heal.

So, why is knowing and thinking about God important? We were not made to think more good thoughts about ourselves. We were made to find life and peace when we think less about ourselves and more about our Creator.

Have You Met Jesus?

If you have never received Jesus into your life or trusted Him for the forgiveness of your sins, I'm going to share with you the *simple* way you can follow Jesus.

Trusting Jesus is as simple as believing and praying these things:

God, I am a sinner. I need a Savior. And I believe, Jesus, that You are the answer to that, that You are the one with the power to forgive sins. I believe that You came to earth, that You paid for sin so that You could rescue me from it. I believe You paid the price for that sin in laying down your life. I believe that You are the Son of God and that on the third day, You rose from the grave, and You are seated beside the Father right now. I want You, and I want to follow You. I want to be in heaven with You one day. I believe that is possible because of Your sacrifice. So I'm in!

That's it, guys. It's as simple as that. We're sinners, and Jesus paid the price. John 3:16 says, "For God so loved the world, that he gave his only Son, that whoever believes in him should not perish but have eternal life."

This is our hope. It is secure. There's no other way to the Father but through Jesus. If you're not sure you believe that, just pray this: "Jesus, if You're real, help me. Help my unbelief."

The way to freedom in our minds is believing who we are as adopted children of the King of the universe. When we believe that about ourselves, we think less about ourselves and more about the mission we have been given—to love God and the people God puts in front of us.

Thinking About God: The Mind of Christ

Jesus gives help for every dark thing you struggle with in life. That's true for your thoughts too. We don't need our spiraling thoughts and bad feelings to just stop; we need our minds to be *rescued. Changed.* Jesus is our rescuer.

- *Do you feel like your thoughts are holding you in chains, like a prison?*
  → Jesus is a rescuer.
- *Do you feel crushed by big things?*
  → Jesus is strong and can lift the weight.
- *Do you feel like your feelings leave you in the dark sometimes, and you don't know where to turn?*
  → Jesus turns on the light.
- *Do you feel like sometimes you don't like who you're turning into?*
  → You can be transformed. Jesus makes you a new creation.

Jesus, You saved me and made the way for my freedom. Thank You for making it possible to free my mind from the thoughts and spirals that pull me down. Thank You for making a way to rescue me!

Power Tool 3
Verses and Powerful Truth for Your Fight

WE ALL NEED HELP REMEMBERING THE TRUTH AS WE WORK to reclaim our minds. May I remind you? Imagine me putting my hands on the sides of your face and looking into your eyes. Here are some things God says about who *He* is and some things He says about who *you* are.

God has declared these truths about Himself and about you. All these things are true for you and for anyone who loves and follows Jesus. This is who we are because of *whose* we are. Our God doesn't change, and He always delivers on His promises.

For When You Need to Remember God Is Bigger

I AM WHO I AM. (Exodus 3:14)

I am the First and the Last. I am the beginning and the end. (Revelation 22:13, NLV)

I am light; in Me there is no darkness at all. (See 1 John 1:5)

My hand laid the foundation of the earth, and my right hand spread out the heavens; when I call to them, they stand forth together. (Isaiah 48:13)

For When You're Feeling Misunderstood

Before I formed you in the womb I knew you. (Jeremiah 1:5)

For When You Feel Ashamed or Struggle with Perfectionism

I chose you and appointed you that you should go and bear fruit and that your fruit should abide, so that whatever you ask the Father in my name, he may give it to you. (John 15:16)

I am he who blots out your [mistakes] . . . and I will not re-member your sins. (Isaiah 43:25)

I will equip you for every good work I've planned. (See Hebrews 13:21)

I will build my church [through you], and the gates of hell shall not prevail against it. (Matthew 16:18)

For When You're Feeling Lonely or Overwhelmed

To all who receive Me, who believe in My name, I give the right to become children of God. (See John 1:12)

Do you not know that you are God's temple and that God's Spirit dwells in you? (1 Corinthians 3:16)

I will put my Spirit within you. (Ezekiel 36:27)

I will not leave you. (See Deuteronomy 31:8)

For When You're Feeling Anxious

I did not give you a spirit of fear but of power, love, and self-control. (See 2 Timothy 1:7)

I will comfort you. (Isaiah 66:13)

I will teach you what is true and help you remember everything I said. (See John 14:26)

I am coming soon. (Revelation 3:11)

My steadfast love endures forever and ever. (See Psalm 138:8)

In just a little while I am coming. (See Hebrews 10:37)

I will come again and will take you to myself, that where I am you may be also. (John 14:3)

For When You Need Hope

You will inherit the earth. (See Psalm 25:13)

You will be with Me. I will wipe every tear from your eyes, and death will be no more.
(See Revelation 21:3–4)

Behold, I am making all things new. (Revelation 21:5)

My kingdom is coming. My will will be done on earth as it is in heaven. (See Matthew 6:10)

. . .

If you need some encouragement today, try saying some of these verses out loud, and write your favorites on a sticky note or type them into your phone—wherever you can see them regularly.

When You're Feeling Anxious

God has redeemed my life, and He can renew my mind.
I can grab one thought—I have a choice.
In Christ, my thoughts can be redeemed.
I can choose what is true over "what if."
I can choose peace and stillness over distraction.
God is good, even if the worst happens.
I can share God exactly where I am today.
When I stay close to Jesus, He will overflow through me.
God is my rescuer and ultimate healer.

When You're Feeling Ashamed

I do not have to fix myself because Jesus died to make
   me right with God.
I choose to believe that God is with me, He's for me,
   and He loves me.
God is with me and beside me, and He will never
   abandon me.
My identity is secure in God.
God will redeem everything that happens to me.
In Jesus, I am fully known and accepted.
I am a child of God.

Even when I fail, God won't leave me or give up on me.
I can choose the mind of Christ.
Focusing on Jesus renews my mind.

When You're Feeling Lonely

I am safe with God. He likes me and wants a relationship with me.
Only Jesus can truly satisfy my longing heart.
I can choose to believe the best in others.
I can experience the joy of self-forgetfulness when I serve others.
I choose to risk being known.
I was created to be seen and loved.
People aren't perfect, and neither am I, but I can choose connection.
I can be bold and brave enough to go first with other people.
I will risk being vulnerable.
Only God can meet my deepest needs.
God built me to need people in my life.

When You're Feeling Overwhelmed

My heart was made to be still before God.
I'm not a victim to my thoughts. I can interrupt them.
The Enemy is real, but my God is stronger.
I can trust God and His truth when I don't know what to do.
I can choose the thoughts I feed and where I direct my energy.
I can choose to spend time in the truth of God's Word.
I can protect my joy by guarding my inputs.

Stillness with God rewires my perspective.
My small choices matter.
When I serve, I come alive.
I am not helpless against the Enemy; Jesus will always win.
I don't have to be enough, because God is.

When You're Feeling Misunderstood or Like Everything's Unfair

In Christ's power, I have authority over my mind.
I can redirect my thoughts by fixing my mind on Jesus.
God will give me what I need when I need it.
God is fighting for me.
It's never too risky for me to choose hope.
When I choose gratefulness, I stop the spiral of negative thoughts and feelings.
Because of Jesus, I can choose to see the good around me despite my circumstances.
I can choose to look for unexpected gifts even when I'm not where I want to be.
Jesus is enough, so I can rest today.
I can trust God to be God and deliver all I need.

When You're Feeling Like a Failure or Struggling with Perfectionism

I am strong, worthy, and loved by the One who created me.
I will choose today to dwell on God's truth.
I am not defined by my worst or best. I am defined by God.
I can use the weapons God gives to win this fight.
I flourish when I draw near to God.

God continues to give me fresh starts.
I don't need to be awesome, because Jesus is.
My struggles in life do not define me.
My thoughts can give life to others.

Visit www.jennieallen.com/kids for more resources!

Acknowledgments

Thank you to my WaterBrook team for helping this get into the world!

And thank you to Jen McNeil, Sarah Rubio, and Laura Wright for editing this book into something so helpful.

I'm blessed to be surrounded by a great team on every side!

Notes

Chapter 2: You Are Not Alone

1. Cristina Sevadijon, "Practical Help for Kids from Psychologist Dr. Cristina Sevadijon," interview by Jennie Allen, May 14, 2020, in *Made for This with Jennie Allen,* podcast, www.jennieallen.com/blog/practical-help-for-kids-from-psychologist-dr-cristina-sevadijon.

Chapter 3: For When You Think . . . *Terrible Things Are Going to Happen*

1. *Britannica Kids,* s.v. "anxiety (*n.*)," https://kids.britannica.com/kids/search/dictionary?query=anxiety.
2. Tim Newman, "Anxiety in the West: Is It on the Rise?," Medical News Today, September 5, 2018, www.medicalnewstoday.com/articles/322877.php.
3. Based on a conversation from Jennie Allen and David Marvin, "Get Out of Your Head (with Special Guest Jennie Allen)" (Dallas, Tex.: Watermark Community Church, November 10, 2020), video shared by *The Porch,* www.theporch.live/messages/7890-get-out-of-your-head.
4. Don Joseph Goewey, "85 percent of What We Worry About Never Happens," HuffPost, updated December 6, 2017, www.huffpost.com/entry/85-of-what-we-worry-about_b_8028368;

quoted in Robert L. Leahy, *The Worry Cure: Seven Steps to Stop Worry from Stopping You* (New York: Three Rivers, 2005), 18–19.

5. Priscilla Shirer and Chrystal Evans Hurst, "Giving Kids Your Presence with Chrystal Evans Hurst and Priscilla Shirer," interview by Jennie Allen, May 28, 2020, in *Made for This with Jennie Allen*, podcast, www.jennieallen.com/blog/giving-kids -your-presence-with-chrystal-evans-hurst-and-priscilla-shirer.

Chapter 4: For When You Think . . . *I Am the Worst*

1. Adapted from *Merriam-Webster*, s.v. "shame," www.merriam -webster.com/dictionary/shame.

2. Amber Elliott, "The Impact of Shame," The Child Psychology Service CIC, https://thechildpsychologyservice.co.uk/theory -article/the-impact-of-shame.

3. Brené Brown, "Shame vs. Guilt," Brené Brown (website), January 15, 2013, https://brenebrown.com/articles/2013/01/15 /shame-v-guilt.

4. Curt Thompson, *The Soul of Shame: Retelling the Stories We Believe About Ourselves* (Downers Grove, Ill.: InterVarsity Press, 2015).

Chapter 5: For When You Think . . . *I Really Wish They Liked Me*

1. Tim Keller, *The Reason for God: Belief in an Age of Skepticism* (New York: Penguin Random House, 2008), 224.

2. Adapted from *Merriam-Webster*, s.v. "toxic," www.merriam -webster.com/dictionary/toxic.

3. This is a synthesis of ideas I discussed with John Townsend: "When You Need to Set Boundaries," interview by Jennie Allen, August 7, 2019, in *Made for This with Jennie Allen*, podcast, www.jennieallen.com/podcast.

Chapter 6: For When You Think . . . *I Have No Control*

1. Adapted from Rebecca Louick, "5 Ways to Help Children Focus on What They Can Control," Big Life Journal, Septem-

ber 17, 2021, https://biglifejournal.com/blogs/blog/help -children-focus-on-what-they-can-control.

2. Louick, "5 Ways to Help Children."
3. Example taken from Cristina Sevadijon, "Practical Help for Kids from Psychologist Dr. Cristina Sevadijon," interview by Jennie Allen, May 14, 2020, in *Made for This with Jennie Allen,* podcast, www.jennieallen.com/blog/practical-help-for -kids-from-psychologist-dr-cristina-sevadijon.
4. Louick, "5 Ways to Help Children."
5. Louick, "5 Ways to Help Children."
6. Louick, "5 Ways to Help Children."
7. William Stixrud and Ned Johnson, "Children Need a Sense of Control," Parents League of New York, March 31, 2020, www.parentsleague.org/blog/children-need-sense-control.
8. Christopher Bergland, "3 Specific Ways That Helping Others Benefits Your Brain," *Psychology Today,* February 21, 2016, www.psychologytoday.com/us/blog/the-athletes-way/201602 /3-specific-ways-helping-others-benefits-your-brain.

Chapter 7: For When You Think . . . *It's Not Fair*

1. Adapted from Kiddle Encyclopedia, s.v. "Justice Facts for Kids," https://kids.kiddle.co/Justice.
2. See Proverbs 31:9; Micah 6:8; Luke 18:7.
3. "What Is Bullying," StopBullying.gov, www.stopbullying.gov /bullying/what-is-bullying; Tim Keeter, "Parenting and the Bullied Child," interview by Samuel Stephens, November 13, 2019, in *Truth in Love,* Association of Certified Biblical Counselors, podcast, https://biblicalcounseling.com/resource -library/podcast-episodes/til-232-parenting-and-the-bullied -child.
4. Acts 9:23, 29; 13:50; 14:5, 19; 15:5, 39; 16:22–23, 39; 17:5–7, 13–14, 18; 21:27–30; 22:24; 23:33–27:2; 27:41–28:1; 28:3–5, 14–16.
5. Julie A. Ross, "When Children Feel Misunderstood," Parent- ing Horizons, www.parentinghorizons.com/node/139.
6. *The Britannica Dictionary,* s.v. "humble," www.britannica .com/dictionary/humble.

Chapter 8: For When You Think . . . *I'm a Failure*

1. Adapted from *Merriam-Webster*, s.v. "perfectionism," www
   .merriam-webster.com/dictionary/perfectionism.
2. This idea is explored in Brené Brown, *The Gifts of Imperfection: Let Go of Who You Think You're Supposed to Be and Embrace Who You Are* (2010; repr., Center City, Minn.: Hazelden, 2020).
3. This is based on Brené Brown's "in the arena" idea, found in Brené Brown, *Rising Strong: How the Ability to Reset Transforms the Way We Live, Love, Parent, and Lead* (London: Vermillion, 2015), loc. 332, Kindle.
4. Simone Marie, "6 Ways to Help Your Perfectionist Child Find Balance," PsychCentral, last updated August 20, 2021, https://psychcentral.com/health/ways-to-help-your -perfectionist-child-find-balance.
5. Isaiah 41:10.

Chapter 9: Inputs

1. Jay Rai, "Why Deep Breathing Relaxes Your Brain," *Forbes,* March 3, 2021, www.forbes.com/sites/forbescoachescouncil /2021/03/03/why-deep-breathing-relaxes-your-brain; Abria Blount, "Deep Breathing Helps Ease Anxiety," PsychCentral, June 30, 2021, https://psychcentral.com/anxiety/why-deep -breathing-helps-calm-anxiety.
2. Amanda MacMillan, "Why Instagram Is the Worst Social Media for Mental Health," *Time,* May 25, 2017, https://time.com/4793331/instagram-social-media-mental -health.
3. Adapted from *Merriam-Webster*, s.v. "meditate," www .merriam-webster.com/dictionary/meditate.
4. Points adapted from Jennifer O'Donnell, "Help Your Tween Deal with Volatile Emotions," Verywell Family, August 31, 2021, www.verywellfamily.com/tweens-and-mood-swings -3288039.
5. O'Donnell, "Help Your Tween."

6. Stephanie A. Sarkis, "Watching Violent News Video Can Be Hazardous to Your Health," *Psychology Today,* October 2, 2017, www.psychologytoday.com/intl/blog/here-there-and-everywhere/201710/watching-violent-news-video-can-be-hazardous-your-health.

LOOKING FOR MORE?

FOR VIDEOS, BLOG POSTS, AND TONS OF FREE DOWNLOADS, GO TO:

JENNIEALLEN.COM